HOW
TO BE
YOURSELF

SIMON DOONAN

HOW
TO BE
YOURSELF

**LIFE-CHANGING ADVICE
FROM A RECKLESS
CONTRARIAN**

INTRODUCTION

Why did I write this book? I had no choice. After becoming aware of a specific and very terrifying trend, I felt compelled to act. The issue is simple: social media is obliterating our priorities.

Social media increasingly commands us to ignore the here and now and to fixate on abstract, far-in-the-future stuff like hopes, aspirations, and dreams. Every time I glance at my phone, I find myself barraged with third-rate advice, deranged encouragements to "believe in your dreams" or "follow your dreams." Dreams? Like what? The one in which I am stuck in an elevator with my grandmother and she is eating her own hair while offering me a sticky bun? Newsflash: Dreams are not to be trusted. Dreams are just nightmares with better furniture. In lieu of focusing on dreams, you must, I beg you, focus on your self. If you

Introduce yourself to...yourself.

have neglected to nurture your true self, your dazzling future accomplishments will afford you no joy. Your self, therefore, is your most precious resource.

Another example of social media's obsession with all those faraway dreams is the concept of the bucket list. Once again, we see the willful ignoring of the now and that same naive fixation on some distant point in the future. In the future, Shirley will scale the north face of the Matterhorn or go zip-lining through a mangrove swamp. In the future— before Shirley dies—she will shag a European soccer player. Yes, I get it, it's nice for old Shirl to have something to look forward to, but if all the really fun stuff is light-years away, who is she going to shag *ce soir*?

So what is it all about, all this dreaming, crystal gazing, and horizon scanning? The answer is simple: it's a sideshow, a distraction from the real work, the heavy lifting, the development of your true self. The excessive focus on that zip-lining future allows you to abdicate responsibility for self-expression and self-development in all areas of your current life. Coming into the now—put down your device, run to the nearest mirror, take a huge deep breath, and stare critically and creatively at your reflection—allows for a full embrace of yourself, right here, right now, warts and all. This is not about worshipping yourself; this is about creating and re-creating yourself. The only surefire way to achieve self-knowledge is to stop wanking around with your life as if it were a series of upcoming, as-yet-unscheduled Instagram posts and to simply explore yourself this instant.

Toss out your bucket list and go climb the Matterhorn today!

Your self is available for bookings. Your self is screaming for attention. Your self is ready to become your most fabulous self.

Ambition and drive are great, but they must be balanced by a solid grounding in the now and the *you*. Beware of allowing your self-esteem to become too enmeshed with notions of prestige and material success, things over which you have limited control. You may or may not be able to achieve your professional and financial ambitions. The one thing that is within your grasp, your control, your vision— is yourself.

The mission of this book is to yank your gaze from the horizon and bring it back to where it belongs: on you and your gorgeous, idiosyncratic, neglect-at-your-peril self.

How dare I?

What on Earth qualifies me, an aging white male, to write a self-help book that includes advice for women? First and foremost, let it be known that I am wildly pro-woman. In fact, I myself am frequently mistaken for one. Strangers often assume, based on a peripheral glimpse of a petite figure in the flowery shirt with the cross-body purse, that they are dealing with a lady. I rarely get through TSA without at least one "Shoes off, *Miss*." (In recent years, this has morphed to *Ma'am* and even *Madam*.)

Secondly, and much more significantly, there's my childhood. My early years forged in me the attitude and independent thinking that now qualify me to machine-gun unsuspecting individuals with advice, edicts, and suggestions. (See the

Blooming boomer.

You can destroy
your now by worrying
about tomorrow.

— Janis Joplin

"Family" chapter.) Nobody in my family gave two shits about what the neighbors thought. Nobody was twee or naff. Nobody complained. Everyone was bold. Having grown up surrounded by unconventional superfreaks, I feel compelled to seek out similar people. I am only truly comfortable when I am around confident eccentrics. I have learned that if I cannot find them, I must create and mold them from whatever raw talent is lurking in my vicinity. Most people can be talked into adopting a more optimistic self-actualized worldview. Some can even be talked into wearing a blue stripper wig.

If a particular individual is being too timid, I feel compelled to draw that person toward the light, with a certain sense of urgency. I am acutely aware of the passing of time. Let me explain: in the '80s, I watched as AIDS decimated an entire swath of pals and colleagues and acquaintances. Even though my friends were cut down in their prime, many had already lived adventurous, imaginative lives. It was as if they had already understood that life is short. Life is for living. Having been gay when it was reviled and illegal, my generation was obliged to self-validate. The lesson: external approval is nice, but do not rely on it.

Armed with resilience and a willful indifference to the judgments of others, I learned how to be—and love—my *self*. So, buckle up! I am now ready to pay it all forward.

Watch your back! The social media culture of likes—weaponized external approval—will snatch the power away from you and put it in the fingertips of others. Resist!

A word of caution before we get started: my natural inclination is to liberate all those I encounter from humdrum conventions and to propel them into a fantasy world by using electrifying edicts in the manner of fashion-empress Diana Vreeland.

Diana Vreeland dug her coral cigarette holder, but, most importantly, she dug herself.

"Unshined shoes are the end of civilization," she professed, and "blue jeans are the most beautiful things since the gondola." I recognize my flaws, and one of them is an addiction to this kind of Vreelandesque hyperbole. Chances are that you grew up in a more conventional milieu. Chances are that you may find these kinds of suggestions jarring or perhaps even off-putting. I have made a strenuous attempt to balance inspirational proclamations with straightforward, useful stuff. In other words: I promise to be helpful.

Here goes with a little helpfulness, right off the bat: I am aware that some readers might find elements of my lingo a tad incomprehensible. For those of you who are baffled by such words as *twee* and *naff*, I have created a Doonan-speak glossary. (See page 154.) Grab the words that resonate with you and make them your own. An idiosyncratic vocabulary is the very opposite of naff.

STYLE

Not long ago, I found myself in Florida staring at a massive iguana—regal, scaly, fluorescent green, otherworldly—and thinking how utterly beautiful it was. "That thing is *disgusting*!" shrieked a glam'd up socialite in Pucci leggings out walking her poodle. I glanced from the strutting pedestrian to the reptile, making a snap comparison. Which one was more beautiful? The Pucci wearer lacked the iguana's effortless confidence. In the beauty stakes, the iguana was definitely the front-runner, simply because it was so fabulously, unapologetically itself.

Reptile, or style influencer, or both?

Beauty is subjective and mysterious, and in the context of this book, it is only a small part of the picture. When you decide to be yourself, to present yourself to the world, you kick-start something much bigger and bolder than mere beauty. It's called...drumroll...*life*!

Yes, ladies and gentleman and transfolk, life begins the moment you decide to be yourself.

Where to start?

Start with the exterior. Start by looking like yourself. #iguana

Looking like yourself sounds like an easy task. It is for an iguana. However, in many cases it involves a certain amount of effort and imagination, a certain investment in time. This is time well spent. Once you establish the outward appearance—the formula, the uniform, the recipe for your

There is almost
nothing outside of
you that will help
in any kind of lasting
way, unless you're
waiting for an organ.

— Anne Lamott

very own look, the look that best expresses your essence—
it gets much easier.

Land on your signature look, and don't be scared to rinse and repeat.

As a kid, I watched my mum get drag'd up every morning, before she charged off to work. Betty Doonan executed her beauty routine—upswept do, '40s red bow lip, plucked and penciled eyebrows, eyeliner, and mascara— with staggering speed and efficiency. With the aid of her cosmetic artistry, well-chosen brassiere, crisp blouse, white pencil skirt, seamed stockings, and a sassy heel, she would transform herself from an average broad into a confident head turner. Mrs. Doonan was a testament to

the Malcolm Gladwell notion that ten thousand hours of practice will result in expertise. Repetition will serve you, dear reader.

Watching Betty go at it, I came to understand that vanity—a frequently and unfairly maligned impulse—can be a life-affirming force, a gesture of creativity and optimism, an antidepressant with no bad side effects. (Conversely, poor hygiene, a ratty coiffure, and a schlumpy outfit are often indications that an

Betty Doonan, hiking in platforms.

individual is struggling.) The desire to invest effort and imagination in your appearance is an adaptive impulse that benefits everyone—a true public service. (More on this later.)

How am I so sure that Betty's outward appearance, the one she orchestrated every day before unveiling herself to the world, was an accurate expression of her intrinsic self? A quick comparison with the other women on our street made it clear that Betty, and Betty alone, was strutting to the beat of her own drum. All the women in our hood looked very similar. The prevailing style mimicked the new queen. (No, not me. I'm referring to the recently crowned monarch Elizabeth II.)

You know that mumsy hairdo with the two curling horns at the front, a twinset and pearls, practical skirts, high-necked blouses and modest "court" shoes. The goal was to avoid appearing attention seeking, or—the biggest crime of all—tarty. As a result, our neighbors looked relentlessly, and similarly, respectable. Only Betty, the uneducated outsider—the lowborn Irish interloper into English respectability—actually dared to be different. Why? Because she *was* different.

The look that Betty created—bold, nonprissy, and memorable, recalling the badass heroines of film noir—was a perfect piece of self-expression. Her inner self and her exterior glam'd-up self were in harmony, two components of a fabulous whole.

Throwing Shade

Betty was a monochromatic lady. Just like those floozies of film noir, she would never be caught dead in baby pink or tango orange. However, color is deeply personal. Maybe black and white bum you out. If you are a chartreuse or fuchsia fanatic, you need to fly your Technicolor flag and proudly declare your affiliations. Ask yourself the following: Which colors make you smile, and which colors make you heave? Which colors tingle your chakras? Which colors are *you*?

Example: I, myself, was once a big fan of chocolate brown. I liked the louche '70s vibration. Then my hair went gray, and my choccie browns lost their luster—gray and brown is very aging squirrel, if you know what I mean—so I switched my allegiance from brown to navy, a lovely adjacency to gray hair. Bam! It worked: I went from a senior squirrel to a silver fox. I often wear my navy duds with bright orange or hot pink. Most of us pick out colors based on mood or context. As the late great fashion designer Pauline Trigère once said, "When you're feeling blue, think red."

The wearing of particular colors is often governed by trends and is not necessarily directly linked to the personality of the wearer. I myself feel indifferent to mauve. However, had I been born in the 1890s—the Mauve Decade, as it is known—I am sure I would have succumbed. Historical hysteria: during the intoxicating era of Oscar Wilde and Marcel Proust, a British chemist named Sir William Henry Perkin was attempting to formulate a treatment for malaria when he accidentally created mauveine, the first synthetic organic dye. The color created a decadent, exhibitionist frenzy among the cognoscenti. Other than demonstrating their susceptibility to fads, the wearing of mauve-hued garments revealed nothing about individual personalities.

Purple/mauve/violet also enjoyed popularity during the years of the '60s counterculture. At the time, I encountered individuals who wore the Royal hue as a way of rejecting conformity and identifying themselves as hippies. In truth, it was just another way of conforming.

While mauve has had moments of polarizing drama, it in no way compares to the provocative complexity of black. Black signifies membership in a gang. Which gang? Take your pick from a staggering array that goes way beyond the film-noir fashions of Betty Doonan: fascists, Sicilian widows, French existentialists, Antifa, punks, nuns, and prelates all respond to the self-dramatizing power of black.

Wearing black can cause bouts of ecclesiastical ecstasy.

Black is now so ubiquitous that it has lost its outsider cred. At one point, it meant you were a radical outlaw; now it means you work at the MAC counter. (Not that there's anything wrong with that.) Certain exceptional individuals have successfully identified themselves with black. Johnny Cash springs to mind. Sticking with your color requires a certain monomania. Even good ol' Johnny allowed himself seasonal lapses: "I wear black because I'm comfortable in it. But then in the summertime when it's hot, I'm comfortable in light blue."

Tom Wolfe is forever remembered as the guy in the white suit. This is because he doggedly stuck with this celestial hue for decades: "My own taste is counter-bohemian. My white suits came about by accident. I had a white suit made that was too hot for summer, so I wore it in December. I found that it really irritated people—I had hit upon this harmless

I imposed black;
it's still going strong
today, for black
wipes out everything
else around.

— Coco Chanel

Tom Wolfe, natty and combative in white.

form of aggression," recalled the author of *The Bonfire of the Vanities*. Wolfe's white suits made him a target for boozing macho types like Norman Mailer, who called out Wolfe's effete dandyism in an attempt to discredit him. Wolfe enjoyed the badinage, and the resulting attention.

Wolfe's whites expressed his desire to kick against the conventions of the literati. Others have used the wearing of white garments to demonstrate their commitment to peace and mindfulness: John and Yoko, Gandhi, and the jewelry designer Kazuko Oshima. In political circles today, the coordinated wearing of all white is a nod to the women's suffrage movement, as exemplified by Alexandria Ocasio-Cortez and her fellow Dems in the United States Congress.

Meanwhile, over on Seventh Avenue: Betsey Johnson's lifelong commitment to hot pink has helped create her memorable persona and fueled the growth of a successful business. She's been hot pinking it since the '60s when she made clothes for Edie Sedgwick, Twiggy, and Julie Christie: "I was born with hot pink blood in my veins. Hot pink is Pow! Sexy! Strong! Alive! Very happy! Loud + proud!" For Betsey, hot pink is every bit as empowering and meaningful as white was to the Suffragettes.

Caution: self-identifying with a color is a hard row to hoe. Be prepared to hoe that hue for decades. It is often necessary to verbally remind people about your chosen color, especially if the color you have chosen is not hot pink but a more subtle hue. Elsie de Wolfe, a towering aesthete of the twentieth century, expressed herself through her love of beige and reminded the world at every opportunity. On first seeing the Parthenon, the legendary interior decorator is said to have screamed, "It's beige! My color!"

Betsey Johnson proselytizes pink-power.

If the Glove Fits, You Must Buy It

Since your body is the most primal thing that you possess—what is more you than your own arrangement of flesh and blood?—it makes sense to give thought and careful consideration to the fit of your garments. The ability to emphasize certain aspects of your body, and to deemphasize others, is written into the US Constitution. OK, it's not, but we all know that it should be.

Perfect fit is the ultimate high.

Edith Head once said, "Your dresses should be tight enough to show you're a woman and loose enough to show you're a lady." Yes, this advice contains sexist overtones of the last century, but the significance and power of a form-fitting garment remains undeniable. Feel free to flip it to

You don't need fashion designers when you are young. Have faith in your own bad taste. Buy the cheapest thing in your local thrift shop—the clothes that are freshly out of style with even the hippest people a few years older than you. Get on the fashion nerves of your peers, not your parents....

— John Waters

your advantage. If you passionately wish to avoid being mistaken for a boring, respectable individual, then be sure to strut around in extremely tight clothing 24/7. The takeaway: your silhouette, the fit of your clothes, can speak volumes, or minimize volumes.

There are no hard-and-fast rules. Fit can signify different things in different contexts. The one great truism: if a garment fits well—I'm thinking in particular of shoulder seam, sleeve length, and waist rise—you, the wearer, will experience a physical pleasure that is sensual bordering on orgasmic. Find a skilled tailor in your neighborhood, and

Violet Chachki throws a perfect fit.

always remember his/her/their birthday. Drop off a ham on Christmas.

As an undersized individual, I prefer a nifty, tailored fit. The last thing I need is yards of fabric wafting about my person and turning me into MC Hammer, or Mrs. Roper. Were I larger, and female, I would seek the comfort of loose caftans, but I would definitely mix it up with the occasional halter top. My pal Ann Ogden, a fashion luminary who designed for Lane Bryant, once shared the following plus-size tip: "If a big chick wears a muumuu, she invariably looks like

Angela Davis's legendary Afro hairstyle speaks volumes.

a mountain. A halter top actually bisects and minimizes her upper torso, and we plumper girls have gorgeous arms."

Hairs to the Throne

The accessory with the most potential for true self-expression is found on top of your head. Imagine pop megaminstrel Ed Sheeran without his hair. He would not be Ed Sheeran. He *is* his hair. His persona—unpretentious, uncontrived, unglamorous, relatable, and unimaginably talented—is perfectly expressed in that untended ginger bird's nest. The same can be said for Albert Einstein, Angela Davis, Sia, and Carrot Top. They *are* their hair. Hairdressers, therefore, are the shamans in the looking-like-yourself movement. They are positioned to guide you toward a look that best expresses yourself.

More important than your clothing choices, your chosen hairstyle is the ultimate playground for self-expression and self-identification.

While the swinging miniskirt-wearers of the '60s ratted and sprayed their bouffants, Iris Murdoch—novelist, academic, and philosopher—wore her hair in a pageboy style. This willfully antiglamourous look gave her gravitas in the male-dominated world of letters and expressed the bookish eccentricity that was such a huge part of her blue-stocking personality. One can imagine a conversation with her hairdresser:

Iris Murdoch's super-bowl haircut.

Hairdresser:	Since you are such a brainiac—too busy thinking profound thoughts to go to the salon—let's make it look like you cut it yourself.
Murdoch:	I often do, around a pudding bowl.
Hairdresser:	Not surprised.

While hair is a great canvas for personal expression, there is a limit to the assumptions that can be made based on the chosen style. Even though they have the same short, stylish, silvery coiffure, the European Central Bank's Christine Lagarde and the Green Party's Jill Stein sit at opposite ends

Who wore it better? Frida or Yulia?

of the ideological spectrum. The hairdo does not tell us much about their personalities. It is more of a marketing device, a PR memo communicating the notion of competence, caring, and efficiency. It also says, "Hello! I'm a modern intelligent woman."

Lagarde and Stein are not the only hair icons with differing ideologies to adopt the same look. I am thinking of Frida Kahlo and the Ukrainian power blonde Yulia Volodymyrivna Tymoshenko, the bohemian artist versus the businesswoman turned politician. Are their hairdos really reflections of their true selves? What do they have in common? By adopting the folkloric crown-braid, these two women expressed their solidarity with the people. Both women were imprisoned: Kahlo was held captive by her physical injuries and her masochistic relationship with Diego Rivera; Tymoshenko was slung into jail after a successful smear campaign, orchestrated by none other than Paul Manafort on behalf of a rival Ukrainian politician. Both were revolutionaries: Tymoshenko co-led the so-called Orange Revolution before becoming the Ukraine's first female prime minister in 2005. Tymoshenko is a post-Communist

Know first, who you are; and then adorn yourself accordingly.

— Epictetus

capitalist, while Kahlo was an old-school Communist, painting a hammer and sickle on her body cast. Two of her final creations, painted in 1954, were titled *Marxism Will Give Health to the Sick* and *Self-Portrait with Stalin*. Both women deserve a BETTY (Doonan) Award. Why? For being every bit as flawed and fabulous as their hairstyles suggest.

Culture is peppered with examples of individuals who managed the Betty feat: they actually look like themselves. These heroes should be celebrated for their panache and their authenticity. In a culture where all kinds of masochistic, costly fakery—hair extensions, boob jobs, ass implants, rib removals, facial fillers, and Botox—have become the norm, looking like yourself is starting to seem like an award-worthy accomplishment. *Et voilà!* The BETTY Awards.

B-E-T-T-Y
Bold Expressive Twinkly and Totally Yourself

Heroes of Style
In the fancy-pants world of interior decorating, there are men who wear silver-gray silk-shantung suits, custom shirts, and foppish foulards during office hours and when lunching with clients. But when the sun goes down, they undergo a macho metamorphosis, donning biker leathers and rugged denims. This syndrome is affectionately known as "chintz by day, chaps by night." This kind of radical, some might say "schizophrenic," costume change recalls the Roman emperor Nero, who would throw off his royal toga and drag up as a hooker, meandering the back alleys of Rome under the cover of darkness, seeking kink and degradation. The goal is clearly to create a parallel self, a self who gets to do naughty things. Managing two selves can be stressful and is hardly a pathway toward mental health. Look at what happened to Nero: he murdered his mother and then fiddled while Rome burned.

But let's put matricide aside and call out stylish individuals who have kept it simple and scored a bull's-eye.

Young Thug, rapping fashion legend.

These people—BETTY Award winners, all!—have figured out one single, uncompromising look that perfectly reflects and integrates all aspects of their personae. Stylish, iconic, and authentic, this wide-ranging group includes people like Bill Cunningham, Lena Dunham, Keith Richards, Angela Merkel, Meghan Markle, Adele, Sasha Velour, Chip and Joanna Gaines, Emmanuel Macron, Whoopi Goldberg, and Diane Keaton—individuals, incidentally, who have had a huge influence on the styles of others. It skews older because young people—the Justin Biebers and Katy Perrys of the world—are still seeking their true selves; as a result, they experiment and change their looks and are hard to keep track of.

A BETTY Award should surely go to rapper and fashion devotee Young Thug. He is the antithesis of chintz by day, chaps by night. He is always, regardless of the hour, relentlessly and fabulously himself. If clothing is nonverbal communication, Young Thug's appearance speaks loudly, and says, "I am an unstoppable creative bad boy who celebrates style, fantasy, opulence, and decadence."

Young Thug has taken the sartorial vocabulary built by Run-DMC, and embellished by Snoop Dogg, 50 Cent, and subsequent hip-hop icons, and run with it. The rapper wears a bewitching mélange of avant-garde designer items mixed with street-style cartoony garments, including maxi cardigans, vivid kagools, and provocative hoodies, accessorized with dreads, ink, extreme eyewear, and mountains of twinkly diamond necklaces and rings. Despite the massive amount of fashionable adornment, Young Thug, who also goes by Jeffery, always seems down-to-earth and totally at one with his finery: "I am fashion," Young Thug told a reporter in 2018. "I don't think I can even get in no deeper. I wake up and breathe this."

Also waking and breathing fashion is *Vogue* editor in chief Anna Wintour—the bob, the shades, the high-necked, short-sleeved printed designer dress, the statement necklaces, the Manolo Blahnik heels—a veritable beacon of modish creative competence, inside and out. The titular

Anna and Karl, infinitely recognizable, eternally themselves.

head of US fashion, Met Ball impresario, Condé Nast deity, cultural barometer, Anna Wintour is one of the most successful people in the history of La Mode. And she dresses the part. I would describe her style as having a base note of power chic, with a top note of intelligent flamboyance.

Like fellow fashion luminaries Tom Ford, Donatella Versace, and the late Karl Lagerfeld, Anna Wintour has the wisdom to stick with the same look. As a result, she not only looks like herself, she also enjoys global recognition. Sticking with the same look, especially in the whirligig of the fashion world, takes courage and nerves of steel, but the dividends are massive. Recognition and iconic status will never be yours if you keep road testing new styles. (I'm exaggerating slightly—as that other iconic *Vogue* editor Diana Vreeland once said, "Exaggeration is my only reality.")

Jean-Paul Sartre and Simone de Beauvoir, like Ms. Wintour and Mr. Thug, are also prime examples of individuals who were, head to toe, inside and out, unapologetically and consistently themselves. Jean-Paul and Simone's refusal to adhere to convention permeated every aspect of their lives, most especially in their dandified beatnik

Jean-Paul and Simone enjoy an existential beverage break.

style. They walked the walk, all the way to the Café de Flore and back to the Sorbonne, smoking furiously all the way.

De Beauvoir's commendable sense of urgency echoes my own at the very beginning of this book. She once said, "Change your life today. Don't gamble on the future, act now, without delay." I just know that Simone and I would have seen eye to eye on the idiocy of dreams and bucket lists. *Je n'aime pas les bucket lists.* I can almost hear her saying it.

Another major area of agreement: the randomness of things. The idea that everything in life is contingent and unpredictable is the central tenet of their existentialist philosophy and has always made sense to me. This is the polar opposite of the contemporary notion—it pops up on dumb reality shows with frightening regularity—that *everything happens for a reason.* If everything happens for a reason, where does that leave people who have actually experienced real tragedy? Tsunamis? Chernobyl? Jean-Paul Sartre was correct: there is no grand plan. Nothing happens for a reason. Everything just happens.

Life is random. Don't waste time looking for patterns where there are none.

Aliens from Planet Batshit

Every few years, a meteor blasts into our orbit and deposits a superfreaky individual from another galaxy. This person sports a totally jarring insane look that says, "I am totally innovative and quite possibly unhinged. Deal with it." Are they really as bonkers and unconventional as they appear to be, or are they merely fronting? Most are fronting. Most are nice people wearing strange garb (see Lady Gaga). Nothing wrong with a bit of packaging: it's a big part of show business. But there are a few special individuals who turn out to be every bit as strange and unique as they appear. The inside

There's people out there saying, "Dress like a girl for once! Wear tight clothes, you'd be much prettier and your career would be so much better!" No it wouldn't. It literally would not.

— Billie Eilish

Billie Eilish, rule-breaking, nail-breaking, street-style avatar.

matches the outside. The drapes match the carpet. Examples include David Bowie, Björk, Missy Elliott, Amy Winehouse.

These aliens keep coming: one of the more recent additions to this genre is Billie Eilish. The *New York Times* described her appearance as "performatively dead eyes (bored, at best), hair dyed in shades of electric blue and pale purple, an all-baggy anti-silhouette—a collective middle finger to the strictures of teen-pop sex appeal."

Her willingness to wear objectively unflattering outfits makes her a style revolutionary, the death knell to the porno-chic movement that has dominated pop culture since the '90s. Her look embodies the disaffection and alienation of youth while leading a charge into a future in which "hotness" is no longer the Holy Grail and individuality rules. She is every inch the creative virago she appears to be.

The most powerful and authentic style statements are made far, far, far away from the red carpet and the runways of Paris.

The Anti-Influencers

What do Nick Offerman, Susan Boyle, Samuel Beckett, and Princess Anne have in common? Reluctant but fabulous, they are the unwitting heroes of stylish authenticity.

Oblivious to trends and modish expectations, unaided by stylists and advisers, certain individuals dress themselves instinctively and authentically, minus all preconceived notions of chic and glamour. They may be a tad quotidian, but they are fascinatingly so. Bring on the anti-influencers.

Robert Mueller is one such dude. He serves extreme rectitude and Waspy realness. You won't catch him chilling in a leopard jumpsuit. His fabulously old-school style comprises a veritable orgy of Brooks Brothers preppiness: white button-down Oxford shirts, navy suit with a center vent, side-parted steel-gray Kennedy hair. Remarkably unremarkable, devoid of anything tacky or parvenu. The payoff, especially for a lawyer like Mueller, is his aura of timeless credibility and gravitas. Is it part of a cunning strategy? I will wager that he dressed like this when he was five years old. This is who he is.

Boring? Not if you dissect the nuances. His Casio DW-290 sport watch, for example, tells us everything we need to know. His is a life of function and service rather than self-indulgence. He is the anti-Liberace.

Speaking of Lib: in order to resonate, Mueller's style needs a counterpoint. He exists in opposition to lads such as Liberace (RIP), Conor McGregor, and Adam Lambert. These flashy, fur-wearing exhibitionist dandies are seen as decadently breaching boundaries of good taste, and we love them for it. Elton John, Floyd Mayweather, Dolly

Conor McGregor, with his man furs and rampant ink, is the anti-prep.

Parton, Migos...these pastie-twirling troubadours exist so that Mueller and the other anti-influencers can clutch their pearls and cling to their modest, authentic sense of style. Do the rhinestone cowboys and flashy fashaholics look like themselves? Over time, those rhinestones start to oxidize, the costumery and the inner self seem to merge into a harmonious whole (see Cher).

Skip to My Lou
While trawling the universe in search of those whose external appearances perfectly reflect the uniqueness of their personae, I made an alarming discovery: a significant number of those who caught my attention were named Louis or Louise or Lou. Does their clothing express their personae? Are they worthy of a BETTY Award? Yes and no. But mostly yes. In chronological order we have....

Louis XIV, also known as the Sun King, created a world where appearances were everything. When he famously said, "L'état, c'est moi," I assumed he meant, "Look at the state of

Louis XIV

my wig. It obviously needs a good comb out." But apparently he was declaring that he, Louis, was the state of France. It cannot be denied that he stopped at nothing to make sure that every aspect of his appearance—rouge, red kitten heels, damask coats and breeches, white silky hose, frothy lace mouchoirs—represented the glory of the Bourbon dynasty. Sadly, it failed to represent the hungry masses. Cue the French Revolution and a tracking shot of Louis XVI, the grandson of the Sun King, and Marie Antoinette being dragged off to the guillotine.

Revolutionary sidebar: In the run-up to the French Revolution, the various factions represented themselves with a variety of chapeaux and colored ribbons. *This is who I am!* These symbols of self-identification—black or green rosettes for the aristos, blue and red and white for the sansculottes—could have incendiary consequences, depending on when and where they were worn. In today's culture, we have a similar system whereby people self-identify by wearing red MAGA (Make America Great Again) hats, black Antifa balaclavas, yellow vests, pink pussy hats, or, in the case of the Democratic women of the US Congress, those all white ensembles. Are we headed toward a revolution? Let's bury our heads in the sand, and skip to the next Lou.

Louise Brooks was every inch the wicked flapper she appeared to be. English theater critic Kenneth Tynan described her as "the most seductive, sexual image of Woman ever committed to celluloid. She's the only unrepentant hedonist, the only pure pleasure-seeker, I think I've ever known." Her bobbed hair—the precursor for Anna Wintour's hairstyle—and impudent gaze were a perfect reflection of her life: she broke social mores, slept with Greta Garbo, and married

Louise Brooks

Louis Armstrong

Louise Bourgeois

Louise Nevelson

Lou Adler

Loulou de la Falaise

moguls. She performed in decadent films—*Pandora's Box* is my personal fave—during Germany's Weimar Republic. She was not happy, which makes perfect sense, because she never looked happy.

Louis Armstrong was a kool kat who dressed the part. Suavely attired in a tux or lounge suit, he clutched a pristine white hankie, which he used to mop his brow after blowing on his trumpet. Despite being a proud African American at a time when racism was ubiquitous—to mention nothing of his socially taboo preference for marijuana over whiskey— Louis penetrated the upper echelons of supper-club society and became a part of it. His song "What a Wonderful World" is a good one to play whenever you feel you are losing your grip.

If you don't know yourself, you'll never have great style. You'll never really love. To me, the worst fashion faux pas—is to look in the mirror, and not see yourself.

— Iris Apfel

Artists Louise Bourgeois and Louise Nevelson bore witness to many of the horrors of the twentieth century. Resilient and self-invented, they both managed to scale the Matterhorn of the art world. Each had an idiosyncratic personal style that became part of their respective legends. Like Louis XIV, these women were their own creations.

Madame Bourgeois, petite, mysterious, and black-clad, dressed like a street urchin. The wrinkles of old age that covered her face—no face-lifts or Botox for her—reflected her bold unconventional POV. Unlike her name, she was not bourgeois. Her orphan, sparrowlike appearance was the perfect foil for her work. I am thinking in particular of the gasp-inducing monumental spider—this work is titled *Maman*—that filled the soaring cavern of the Tate Modern in London.

Nevelson, with her gooey fake lashes and towering fur hats, had the appearance of a mythological priestess from *Game of Thrones*. As with Bourgeois, her unique appearance was the perfect counterpoint to her work, which consists of everyday objects—chair legs, moldings, wooden paintbrushes, etc.—arranged and elevated in the manner of religious altars and painted all black or sometimes all white or gold.

Lou Adler, the stratospherically successful media mogul who produced everything from Carole King's *Tapestry* album to *The Rocky Horror Picture Show*, dresses in a fun, willfully infantile way that declares the following: I'm not really a hardheaded business dude or a tough negotiator. I'm really just a creative toddler! That's why I wear oversized white eyewear and a back-to-front Kangol newsie hat.

Does he deserve a BETTY? He looks great; however, since he is using his appearance as a negotiating tactic, he only earns half a BETTY.

Loulou de la Falaise was a chaotic bohemian who made her name working for Yves Saint Laurent. Loulou's job—she was the queen of accessories—was to garnish the rigorous collections of the great Yves with her own nonchalant gypsy style. With daring combinations of materials—ceramic, shells, plastic, cork, and leather—she reinvented the idea of costume jewelry and made a massive contribution to the YSL legend. Her (not well-kept) secret was that she was simply doing Loulou. She was her oeuvre.

A Smidgen of Eccentricity

Full-blown eccentrics can be rather terrifying. A casual dinner with the Marchesa Casati—Italian heiress and art patroness—could conclude with you being munched by her pet panther. Less radical eccentrics—Iris Apfel, Edith Sitwell, Tilda Swinton, Leigh Bowery, Little Edie Beale, or Boy George—are celebrated in our culture with increasing enthusiasm. Social media encourages and rewards idiosyncratic gestures. The pressure is mounting for the average individual to turn up the volume and create an Instagram-worthy personal style. Caution: don't get carried away. There's no point in trying to turn yourself into a Nancy Cunard–type, unless that is who you are. (The Cunard heiress—a poster child for the decadent madness of the decadent '20s—was a stylish extremist who obliterated social norms and wore massive clanking ivory bracelets from wrist to armpit.)

For most people, it's not about unleashing a torrent of eccentric flamboyance. Dressing like yourself involves one simple noteworthy proprietorial gesture. Whoopi Goldberg has her center-parted dreads, and Madeleine Albright has her myriad brooches. A simple signature flourish—a fan, a dangling crystal, a heart, a peculiar cameo pin, a plush velvet headband—is just enough eccentricity to make you visible and memorable. This signature flourish of personal expression could be far more discreet than anything concocted by Virgil Abloh or Rick Owens: it can be as simple as a raspberry beret, a vintage Boy Scout woggle on your

I love baking. That's my look: Aprons—
I have thirty of them—
with high heels.

— Amy Sedaris

Jeff Beck, guitar legend and '60s floral icon.

scarf, a particular manicure, a blue French worker's jacket (see Bill Cunningham, RIP), or even a special word or phrase that you make your own. Examples: Tallulah Bankhead called everyone *daahling*, and drag performer Miss Vanjie adopted the habit of repeating her name while walking backward.

How did my own signature flourish come about? In the swinging '60s, when I was a teen, Mick Jagger, Ray Davies, Jeff Beck, and Brian Jones, my idols, all wore flower-printed button-down shirts made from classic Liberty of London fabric. This androgynous gesture—the preppy shirt in the girly fabric— yanked at something deep in my repressed gay psyche. I wanted one so badly, but I knew it would have been a disaster. In my gritty small-town milieu, wearing a flowery shirt would have revealed far more about myself than was advisable. In fact, it would have been the equivalent of walking into oncoming traffic.

In the '90s, I was strolling through Liberty when I came upon those bolts of flowers and experienced a Proustian déjà vu. Finally I could connect with my teen self without risking violence and derision and unfurl my three-decades-old androgynous impulse. I could exhibit the self that I had been forced to conceal.

And the BETTY Award goes to...*moi*.

PEOPLE

Get in formation. Time for a group hug IRL.

Social anxiety is the new athlete's foot. Young and old, we have become a nation of screen addicts staring anxiously at our phones, experiencing FOMO, gulping down Adderall, sucking on vaping devices, watching porn, playing Candy Crush, and texting each other endlessly about our anxiety disorders. We are living in a dystopian hell of our own making.

So what is the answer?

The answer is simple. Reconnect with yourself and with others, in person. Less screen time and more IRL. Put down your phone, leave the house, and start walking.

Walking Down the Street

Deprived of your phone, you can focus on the important stuff, like developing a signature walk. Start by examining your current walking style. Are you knock-kneed and apologetic? Are you stomping your feet with unexpressed rage? Your gait reveals so much. Take charge of your limbs, and make sure they express some key aspects of your persona.

Sometimes the thing that's weird about you is the thing that's cool about you.

— Maureen Dowd

Caution: brace yourself for negative feedback. Not everyone is going to like your walk. My husband and I, for example, loathe each other's walks. My Jonny waddles down the street at top speed, with his feet pointed out, like an irate duck, often glancing at his phone. I, being older, generally superior, and rather less inclined to obsess about my phone, walk much slower. Drinking in the world around me with a connoisseur's eye, I move at the speed of a '50s couture model, stopping to twirl every now and then to show off some back detail or to check the angle of my chapeau in a shop window reflection.

No balking, or talking—just walking.

For me, hats and walking outside are synonymous. I keep a stack of hats next to the door. Hats are a way to express yourself while you stroll the boulevards or—here comes a heretical suggestion (more on this later)—expressing something other than yourself. Once you are confident that you are inhabiting your best self, it's fun to indulge in a little role-playing. The best example of this deception *au chapeau* occurs in Nathanael West's novel *The Day of the Locust*, in which the protagonist notes the deceptive hat choices of the denizens of Hollywood during the '30s: "The fat lady in the yachting cap was going shopping, not boating; the man in the Norfolk jacket and Tyrolean hat was returning, not from a mountain, but an insurance office; and the girl in slacks and sneaks with a bandanna around her head had just left a switchboard, not a tennis court."

Public Transport

When I ride the A train in New York City, I am always amazed at the diversity of styles on offer. Something about this particular subway line encourages self-expression: women of color with elaborate braids; aging Wall Streeters in threadbare seersucker, and NYU kids wearing avant-garde designer duds. On the A train, people make an effort. As a result, I have never felt overdressed. If anything, I always feel appreciated. This is because fellow riders often compliment me on my noteworthy accessories. Whenever I wear my monogrammed Goyard man bag, I invariably get a "Love your bag. Are you from South Dakota?"

One day the penny dropped, and I realized I should probably make an effort to reciprocate and toss a few compliments at my fellow travelers. (I was suffering from that weird British speak-only-when-spoken-to inertia, plus a bit of narcissism.) So I started giving compliments and quickly realized this was a win-win. When complimenting, I am able to express my tastes while applauding the self-expression of others. In person.

Conclusion: if you choose to ride the subway staring at your phone, you masochistically deny yourself this kind of life-enhancing IRL interaction.

Dining Out

Eating out and being yourself used to be so easy. Now it is an ordeal. It requires that you resist. Why? Because restaurants have declared war on their customers.

Instead of being able to order a basic scrummy meal, you must now submit to an appalling innovation: small shared plates. These Instagram-friendly horrors are concocted by tyrannical chefs who insist on combining improbable ingredients—cuttlefish with mole or chopped fiddlehead

Meat and potatoes = comfort food for the soul.

ferns with sheep's pancreas, soaked in artisanal kumquat oil and covered in red-pepper flakes and locally harvested rock salt—when all you really want is steak and a baked potato. You are at the mercy of some culinary visionary who wishes to inflict his "creative" contrivances on your gastrointestinal tract.

My mother-in-law, Cynthia Adler, is the face of the small-plates resistance movement: she refuses to be tyrannized and orders exactly what she wants, circa 1960. "I'll have a lamb chop with a side of mixed vegetables." It's fun to watch the waiter crumple like the melting Wicked Witch.

Newsflash: the whole point of a menu has always been to satisfy the individual cravings of a diverse group of customers. The whole notion of small sharing plates is, therefore, diametrically opposed to the concept of being yourself. In this new scenario, the only person getting to be themself is the chef. The rest of us are too busy trying not to choke on pepper-crusted rabbit goujons to even think about being ourselves. #resist!

In Someone Else's House

Per Sir Winston Churchill, I am a big believer in reclining whenever possible. For Winnie this was about "economy of effort"; for me this is less about conserving energy and more about minimizing formality. Formality—standing on ceremony for hours as if you are at a constipated Buckingham

Never stand up when you can sit down, and never sit down when you can lie down.

— Winston Churchill

Palace garden party—discourages you, and everyone around you, from being yourself. Sprawling, reclining, and spreading are the key to feeling like yourself and the foundation of a good party. (The only reason people are standing at Holly Golightly's fabulous cocktail party in the movie *Breakfast at Tiffany's* is because, other than the sawn-off bathtub/couch, she has no furniture.)

Sitting down is the great equalizer.

I have a vested interest. The main reason I exhort guests to lounge rather than stand is because I am, as you have probably gathered, a pint-sized charmer. When exuberant guests stand too close, any stray spittle makes a downward arc onto my face and finery.

The greatest legacy of the Roman Empire? The art of lolling and lounging.

If your guests appear not to be enjoying themselves— they have tired of interacting and are sneaking peeks at their phones—then I suggest you haul them back into the moment with what I call the Reynolds Wrap crafting challenge:

Grab a roll of tinfoil from the kitchen, pass it around, instruct each guest to tear off two feet, and challenge them to fashion a nifty headdress. #selfexpression #fashionshow #competition #winneravoidsdishwashingduty

At the Gym

If as a nonconformist you take offense at the sight of acres of people in identical black Lycra, then remember this: it's not mandatory to wear gym clothes to the gym. Feel free to mix it up—vintage soccer jerseys, novelty leprechaun T-shirts, colored swim shorts, star-spangled designer sneakers instead of rigorous workout footwear—and express a personal point of view. For example: at my gym, I have observed a slender older lady who wears elegant men's clothing— high-waisted, pleated Oxford bag pants with crisply ironed button-down shirts, à la Katharine Hepburn—while walking on the treadmill and reading the *New York Times*. She looks like herself.

In recent years, I have amassed a collection of infantile boys' graphic T-shirts, which now form the basis of my gym attire.

Who needs Spandex when you've got a saucy sailor suit?

I am wearing one as I type. It's a bright blue long-sleeved number with a huge tiger's face on the front. The words BE BRAVE are emblazoned across the tiger's chest, and mine.

At a Party

Parties and events are changing radically. Regardless of the occasion—a book-signing cocktail party, the launch of yet another brand of bottled water—you will probably be deaf by the time you leave. Yes, the new trend is to play ear-splitting dance music at nondancing occasions. This creates "atmosphere"—what an exciting bris this must be!—but causes massive confusion among the older attendees who equate loud music with line dancing at Studio 54 or pogoing at the Mudd Club. I am never sure whether I should jiggle my wiggle or cup my hand and yell into my neighbor's ear. How to be yourself at such an occasion? Observe the younger attendees. They have figured it out. If they have something to say, they text each other. In lieu of dancing or chatting, they take iPhone pics of each other. I am not judging, just reporting.

The key to being your most festive self, regardless of the brouhaha around you, is to be informal and comfy. The ultimate way to be comfy at a glam event is to wear pajamas. Choose the pajama based on your personal style. In the '70s, I had a nostalgia-obsessed friend named Irene, a hairdresser who wore slinky, vampy silk Jean Harlow pajamas with boudoir mules to trendy discos. For a less femmy look, go for classic cotton with vertical stripes. Chinese pajamas scream Anna May Wong (that's a good thing). Since I am working through a second childhood in my personal style, I choose goofy printed kid's pajamas. For added comfort, these can be worn with groovy Gucci sneakers. Avoid scuffies, hot-water bottles, and teddy bears. No need to bash people over the head with your Peter Pan theme. You may prefer frilly nighties to flannel jamjams.

Grace Coddington luxuriating in her Louis Vuitton PJ's and matching purse.

Go ahead, twirl your chiffon on the dance floor. Better yet, take it poolside for an unconventional coverup.

On Vacation

Social media has turned travel into a competitive sport. It's rare to open Insta—the ultimate FOMO arena—and not be confronted by an image of a pal proudly preening in front of the temples in Angkor Wat, the Trevi Fountain, that house where giraffes poke their heads through the windows, or snuggling with dolphins. These are the bucket-list locations—the new Disney moments. Make no mistake about it: this is weaponized travel. You get to machine-gun friends and family with your snaps and observations—in real time!—while aggressively reproaching them for never having visited these locations. My questions to Insta-travelers are as follows: How did you actually feel when you were standing in front of the Taj Mahal? Did you really take it in, or were you just framing an artful shot? Are you genuinely interested in seventeenth-century Mughal mausoleums, or were you experiencing a sadistic delight as you contemplated the FOMO you were about to inflict on your followers?

I do think that socializing on the Internet is to socializing what reality TV is to reality.

— Aaron Sorkin

Even more incomprehensible, and just as bucket-listy, is the intrepid stuff: there's your Insta-pal riding a hyena, or about to cough up blood on the side of Mount Everest, or seeking spiritual replenishment and design inspiration in a far-flung mosquito-infested temple or yurt. Great for selfies but not for being/feeling like yourself, especially if you happen not to be the intrepid type. If intrepid is who you are then Airbnb that yurt and have at it. But if you are Stella Staycation, then own your truth, put your feet up, and turn on *Judge Judy*. My point is: don't follow the herd. Don't feel guilty because you have no desire to head over Victoria Falls in a rubber ball. Customize your travel to reflect your idiosyncratic tastes and needs.

Intrepid Instagram posts will garner followers, some friendly, some less so.

If Wildwood, New Jersey, is your Côte d'Azur, then off you go, and please have a fabulous time.

The Meaning of Fun

Being yourself in a social situation is a function of how chillaxed you are, which is, in turn, a function of how much fun you are having. Fun relaxes, and when relaxation occurs, you are more likely to inhabit your true self.

Fun happens when you stop talking and do something with your body and/or hands. Whether it's felting, decoupaging, origami, or making a kid's fort out of multicolored pool noodles, something about the act of making disinhibits the inhibited and allows for the flowering of the self. If you do not feel the siren call of the glue gun, and crafting is not your thing, then how about a dopey tourist attraction? The Kardashians have figured this one out. Yes, they mumble and stare at their devices, but eventually, having bored one another to death, they ride go-carts or pet miniature donkeys and instantly seem so much happier.

On reality TV shows, the participants only start to relate to each other successfully once they stop verbally processing and start playing some inane challenge game, often involving flagellation with pool noodles. This raises the topic of transcendental experiences, about which you will read more in the concluding chapter. For now, please contemplate the following: when it comes to being yourself, a pool noodle can have profound implications.

LOVE

When you are yourself—freewheeling, grooving, moving through life, devoid of neurotic insecurities and neediness— you exude a certain relaxed self-confidence, which is intoxicating. Others get drunk on you. When you are yourself, you are at your most lovable, regardless of the content of your particular self. Even if being a deranged psychopath is your most authentic self, you are lovable to the person who has a penchant for deranged psychopaths.

Hang Out Your Shingle and Mingle

The key to finding *the one* is to stop giving a shit. Lose the desperation. This does not mean that you do not need to make an effort. Au contraire! All the energy previously squandered dealing with your anxieties should be diverted into a vigorous marketing campaign, for yourself. Get the word out, telegraph your availability, charge ahead with your life, but, most importantly, lose the insecurity, or at least make every attempt to mask it. Eventually the fretty feelings will fade away, and all that will be left will be your magnetic self.

Magnetized by Monica Vitti.

In addition to losing your desperation, you must also ditch any grandiose expectations. Andy Warhol once said, "People have so many problems with love, always looking for someone to be their Via Veneto, their soufflé that can't fall." Take a tip from the man with the finger-in-the-socket white fright wig: when looking for love, be prepared to encounter— and reinflate—a few dropped soufflés along the way.

Online dating is your obvious first stop, and yes, there are some inherent problems: the full majesty of you—or that of your prospective partner—is only revealed in person. Online dating, therefore, requires that you communicate your fabulous self, in absentia, via images and the written word. Don't be daunted. Give it a whirl. The plethora of mobile apps—swipe left, swipe right!—vastly increases the statistical probabilities. Walk into a bar and you have access to a few dozen prospects, many of whom will be too busy drowning their *weltschmerz* to even notice you. Join a dating site, on the other hand, and the choices go Ding! Ding! Ding! like a Vegas jackpot.

Writing your profile is something only you can do. Involving family and friends is a disaster. They will bring their own *mishegas* to the table, projecting their own ghastly foibles and disappointments onto you, and send you down a dark and terrible road. Pull out your quill, and treat it like a creative writing project.

When writing your profile, it's OK to amplify certain qualities and turn down the volume on others. #prettylittlelies If you are a reserved person, then try to sound a little more cheeky than usual. If you are a tornado of extroversion, then lower your tone to a quieter bluster. Regarding photos: unless you are a sex worker by profession, keep the pouty hotness factor under control. You don't want people to think you are a hooker or a hustler—unless, of course, you are. *Interested* and *amused* are your *mots du jours*. Better to look interested and amused rather than sexually aroused. Appearing interested and amused is the opposite of resting bitch face. I learned this the hard way after appearing on Eliot Spitzer's short-lived current affairs TV show. Whenever another guest began talking, I switched off completely, and my face collapsed like one of the aforementioned soufflés. "When other guests are speaking, it would be nice if you made an attempt to look interested and amused," hissed the producer. This great advice is seared into my brain.

Though the www gives you access to more individuals who might be the one, it also gives you access to more serial killers and fruitcakes. Conclusion: online dating is worth pursuing, but be prepared to kiss some frogs, hyenas, flopped soufflés, and superfreaks. Once you have identified a nonpsychotic prospect, then set up a date. Choose a place that neither of you have been to before. Try somewhere unexpected. (I myself have not spent nearly enough time in Staten Island and would welcome the opportunity to get to know it a little better.)

A first date screams for matching outfits and an unconventional location.

If the chosen locale turns out to be dire, it will make for a shared experience. The two of you can join forces against the proprietor of the offending bar or restaurant.

Approach this first date with breezy confidence—interested and amused!—safe in the knowledge that there is no such thing as a mishap. For example, my sister and her wife met on a blind date, and they both showed up wearing the same green fleece zippered jacket and fanny pack ("bumbag" in the UK). Awkward? Not so much. Rather than running away, screeching back to their respective nests, they saw the humor in their Patagonias and still laugh about it twenty fleecy years later.

Whether you opt for a drink, a coffee, or a full-course dinner, try to remember that etiquette and table manners are horribly overrated. Who cares if a person uses the wrong knife or double-dips the fondue? There are, however, a few red flags. Even if you look like Gisele Bündchen or Tom Brady, masticating with your mouth open is objectively repulsive.

If open-mouthed mastication does start to occur, or if you start to get bad stalker vibes from your date—you suddenly see yourself floating facedown off the coast of Fort Lauderdale on an episode of *Dateline*—then bring the date to a screeching halt. You can accomplish this simply and swiftly by acting like an insane person. Do a total Blanche Dubois. I find that people, even die hard stalkers, have a distinct aversion to the mentally ill. Your dodgy date will flee the scene, never to be heard from again.

Assuming that things go well, however, your next step will be to reach out post-date, asap. I once screwed this up, royally. After my first date with my now husband Jonathan Adler, I failed to follow up. I assumed based on our fourteen-year age difference that he thought I was a boring old fart, and I never bothered to call. Then, by chance, I ran into the yenta who had orchestrated the date. "Why the hell haven't you called him? He really liked you. You blew it. He's probably with somebody else by now," admonished my pal.

I just never had that
thing with women.
I would do it silently.
Very Charlie Chaplin.
The scratch, the look,
the body language.
Get my drift?
Now it's up to you.
"Hey, baby" is just not
my come-on.

— Keith Richards

At that moment, as I went barreling toward the nearest pay phone to make the call, I realized that I really, really liked him, too. Some tragic insecurity in my soul needed to hear that he liked me before I could feel anything. In other words, there's something horribly wrong with me, and I should probably not be doling out relationship advice to others.

Real men wear orchids.

How to Get Serious

The whole notion of courting is rather old school, which might not be such a bad thing, depending on the individual. Showing up in a convertible, clean and scrubbed, clutching flowers and bonbons definitely has novelty value. This approach, however, is not something you can try for ironic kicks. It needs to be authentic and true to your style.

The conventions associated with courtship and expressions of love—I refer to heart-shaped boxes of See's candy, long-stemmed roses, anniversaries, trips to Tiffany's—are great for the economy...but are they great for *you*? Are they great for anyone? The answer is yes! Some people eagerly devour all the conventional props and gewgaws of romance, the flutes of champagne and the choccie-dipped strawbs.

If you are appalled by these clichés, that's fine, too. But you have to find alternatives. It's not enough to sneer at the corny stuff. It is incumbent on you to come up with some ideas of your own. Deviating from the norm requires effort and imagination. When it comes to falling in love, you must find a way to do love that best expresses you.

Example: My husband and I are both irreverent and unresponsive to the ditzy conventional stuff. In lieu of sentimental heart-shaped tchotchkes and frilly missives, we create our own. We buy romantic cards from the pharmacy—the more corny and traditional the better— and deface them and tweak the sentiments, inserting insulting and appalling language. This makes us laugh and further cements our bond.

A shared sense of humor is a good augur, but not a 100 percent guarantee. The truth is that successful relationships come in all shapes and soufflés, and, as a result, there is no way to predict outcomes by reading tea leaves and such. Analyzing your prospects with a particular individual is, therefore, a massive waste of time—time is better spent defacing earnest greeting cards.

If things are evolving organically and in a nonchalant fashion, you have reason for optimism. If steam and passion and excitement are coming out of every orifice, then your romance is probably going to be more of a blowout. Who was it who once said, "Dump trucks are more reliable than freight trains"? Probably the same person who said, "You are less likely to contract the plague on a rusty tugboat than on a big ole luxury cruise ship." Probably me.

It's important not to overintellectualize the process of mate selection. When you are being yourself, you can trust your gut. This is what my parents did. They met one day in a soup kitchen at the end of World War Two. Two months later, after little discussion and minimal introspection, they got married, at a registry office with two chums as witnesses. Then they headed to the pub next door, where they drank vast quantities of alcohol, caroused, and lost the marriage license. They both thought this was hilarious. *Et voilà!* They each met their match. P.S. For the rest of their lives, they never celebrated their wedding anniversary because they

You may depend upon it, that a slight contrast of character is very material to happiness in marriage.

— Samuel Taylor Coleridge

could not locate that marriage license or remember when they had gotten married. Could this be where I got my lack of sentimentality and my aversion to formal occasions?

How to Make It Work

Like my parents, my husband and I have a spectacularly successful relationship. This is because we are infantile, and canine. We act like a couple of dopey Labradors. We have low expectations. We are affable. We do not go in for lots of interpersonal processing. Think Beavis and Butthead.

Betty and Terry's recipe for happiness: low expectations and a lost marriage license.

Some marriages require more Sturm und Drang, just like George and Martha in *Who's Afraid of Virginia Woolf?* Having differing worldviews can make for a spicy relationship. Example: Betty Doonan was a working-class Tory. Terry Doonan was a socialist Labourite. Neither yielded to the other's view. Both remained true to themselves. This added a little frisson of tension, which spiced up their relationship, especially around election time.

Badinage can be fun, but sometimes things get insanely tense and you may need to turn a blind eye to your beloved's opinions and aberrant behaviors. The most effective way to deal with your dissonances and conflicts, whether you are straight or gay, is through teasing. Don't wait till your disgruntlements have made you homicidal. Tease early and often!

Push-up bras, fishnets, sexy heels, plunging décolletages? Yes, you can tease another person with kittenish lingerie, but the best type of teasing—the type of teasing that makes a relationship last decades—involves careful mockery. Taking the piss. Teasing is by far the best way to diffuse tension in a relationship. Gripes tend not to ossify if you address them on a regular basis via teasing. I've found that the best way to tease a loved one is by channeling the family pet. We all invent voices for our pets. Now is your big chance to put yours to use. It's much better for the family pet to tease your loved one for grabbing too many doughnuts than it is for you to do so.

Example: Your partner appears wearing a washed-out green shirt that makes him/her/them look like death. You don't want to say anything because he/she/they bought it, and he/she/they likes it. Your pet comments, "Oh, honey, when did you decide that jade was your color?"

You follow up, in your voice, by castigating the pet for being mean to your SO. Caution: teasing requires a nuanced knowledge of the teasee's foibles. Failure to customize the level of teasing to match the sensitivity of your partner will lead to hurt feelings, which may result in—ugh!—the need to apologize.

Victorian-era British Prime Minister Benjamin Disraeli once said, "Never complain. Never explain." Back when I was a corporate muckety-muck at Barneys in the '80s and '90s I emblazoned

Liberace Adler-Doonan, insult proxy extraordinaire.

People should fall
in love with their eyes
closed. Just close
your eyes. Don't look.

— Andy Warhol

Disraeli's dictate across the door of my office. It was my way of disinviting any potential kvetchers. Regrettably, this era has passed, and it is no longer appropriate to discourage employee whining in this manner. Complaints, admissions of guilt, and groveling apologies are now, unfortunately, enjoying enormous popularity across the entire culture.

Some individuals are natural apologizers. It's part of their nature. Others, such as myself, are obliged to fake it. There is only one way to deliver a fake apology: capitulate, dramatically. If you are busted by a loved one for some perceived infraction—overteasing, for example—respond with an operatic, over-the-top apology. These exaggerated mea culpas are much more effective than tentative ones. If you prostrate yourself with remorse, your loved one is quickly going to wish that you would stop atoning. If you are tentative, your amour will demand more contrition.

If the apology does not work, or maybe if you are simply starting to loathe the other person, you may need to call it quits. Ending even a brief relationship can be challenging and tortuous. Violence is never the answer. Gwyneth Paltrow and Chris Martin were roundly mocked when they advocated "conscious uncoupling," but it's actually a great idea. The key is to end as you went in: totally being yourself.

People stay in gruesome relationships because they are scared of dealing with reality solo. The way around this is to recognize all the benefits of being alone, lying diagonally across the bed and listening to Burt Bacharach's greatest hits while eating Turkish delight being the most obvious. You get to be your most selfish self again!

If the prospect of being alone is keeping you in a crap relationship, you must consciously develop a picture of the single life in which you unleash every demonic impulse that flits through your brain, and then jump ship. Once unencumbered, you can enjoy a few months of Burt Bacharach before leaping back into the fray and seeking a non-crap relationship.

Ditch that turgid dude, and enjoy a self-indulgent singleton lifestyle.

Making It Legal

Getting married is preceded by a proposal. Or is it? My
husband and I never proposed to each other. The mechanisms
of marriage proposal are beyond our comprehension. I cannot
think of anything more hilarious than the sight of either
of us on our knees, clutching a tiny box from Zales, and
staring up imploringly at the other. I don't mean to hate on
this particular convention. It's like getting Botox or riding
a unicycle. A personal decision. Each to his own.

Many of my female friends seem to be waiting for the
mystical moment when their man pops the question. This

seems very archaic. But maybe you are an archaic person, in which case feel free to do things the old-fashioned way.

Closer examination usually reveals—and this observation applies to the entire spectrum from hard-boiled hetero all the way through to LGBTQ—that, paradoxically, the proposee is in the driver's seat. Through a clever series of almost imperceptible cues, the proposee has brought the proposer to the mountaintop. The proposer goes to the altar believing that it was all the proposer's idea.

Popping the question is the easy part. All the overwhelming stuff kicks in once the proposal is accepted and you decide to charge ahead with your wedding. For example, now you are obliged to register. The retailer in me applauds the impulse to purchase mounds of tchotchkes. Spend! Spend! Spend! The nonretailer wants people to refrain from strong-arming cash-strapped relatives to forgo their annual week in Asbury Park in order to buy blenders, gravy boats, and chafing dishes. On a positive note: Weddings are a perfect opportunity for self-expression. A wedding is a manifestation of your personal brand. When it comes to planning the decor, cake, etc., you must ask yourself the following profound question: "How much *szhoosh* is too much szhoosh?"

You should feel free to make your wedding as freaky, opulent, austere, conventional, fabulous, or feral as you are.

This probably comes as a big surprise to many readers who might think of me as "an extremely szhooshy fashion queen," but the reality is that I am unconventional and punk rock in my outlook. My personal preference, therefore, is for feral weddings. Feral weddings can be just as much fun as flashy weddings, if not more. My sister, Shelagh, and her partner,

It is not a lack of love but a lack of friendship that makes unhappy marriages.

— Friedrich Nietzsche

Tall cake-toppers, short grooms.

Anna, had a commitment ceremony—fleece jackets and bumbags a-go-go—that was a total blast but hardly what you would call superposh. After dining, guests were handed trash bags and bussed their own tables. It was so FUN and informal. Can you imagine being at a fancy Kardashian wedding on a Malibu bluff, and having Kris Jenner, out of the blue, hand you a Hefty bag and tell you to snap to it? Brilliant.

My husband and I share a terror of megazhooshy weddings. This is because all the superglam weddings we have attended have led, inexorably and agonizingly, to unglam divorces. If you are the storybook romantic who lives for weddings, then do not let the statistics stop you from going full szhoosh. And if your fantasy $$$ wedding ends in divorce, so what? Look on the bright side: you get to do it all over again—even more szhooshily and over the top than before!—with some new prince or princess charming. Meanwhile, those of us who saved money by having a feral, cheapo wedding will be lolling in a hammock next to Jimmy Buffett.

How you are with your dog remains the gold standard for loving and being loved.

Your Best Married Self
Get canine! Pets rid us of our neuroses, or they at least give it a damned good try. They also accept us, warts and all. If you can replicate the love and acceptance and caring that characterizes your relationship with your dog, you will enjoy an enviable long-term relationship.

Foxylady is a proud rescue mutt. She and I are at our happiest when gamboling in the surf and canoodling on the sand. I show my love by splashing her, drying her with a warm towel, caressing her for hours, and telling her how wonderful she is and how much I adore her. We stare into each other's eyes. At these moments we are our most authentic selves. The exact same scenario works for me and my husbear: gamboling *sur la plage* and toweling and canoodling and not talking too much.

Dogs are much better at communicating their needs—tummy rubs, exercise, food, "please take me out for a walk and a poo"—than people are. Their straightforward neediness is part of what makes them easy to love. Some people are hopeless at articulating their needs. Others are a little too good at it. We can all learn from dogs who manage to do it sans words.

Shelter name: Martha. Real name: Foxylady.

It's important to note that dogs are essentially mute. Yes, they bark, but they never yammer at you and say jarring things like "I'm worried about my brand identity" or "Please tell me that muffin was organic." In this regard we differ from them. If anything, we are the opposite. While our dogs never talk, we, Homo sapiens, cannot stop talking. During the infatuation phase of a relationship, it is good to take a cue from Fido. Silence can be golden.

Final thought: once you have found your truest self, your dance card will fill up, and you will find *the one*. Unfortunately finding love and getting hitched can prove to be quite crazy-making. When you are in the dizzy tizzy of

There is a time for
many words and there
is a time for sleep.

— Homer

being married and trying to make it all work, you are often so wound up that it's hard to be yourself. *Et voilà!* You are back to square one, trying to clarify who you are, but this time in order to stay in love.

This cycle of finding yourself and losing yourself is a natural part of the human condition. Self-clarity waxes and wanes. Yourself is a work in progress. Again, inspiration can come from the canine community for whom breezy resilience is key. When things start getting gnarly, simply wag your tail and chase a ball.

WERK

Once upon a time, before wellness rooms and vegan snack centers....

The workplace of my youth was regimented. This was no accident. Those in charge had either fought in World War One or Two, and they were not about to take any shit from a pushy upstart wearing platform shoes and glam-rock man blouses. This was a time when personal phone calls were verboten, lateness resulted in docked pay, and the boss had carte blanche to put his hand under your crepe de chine.

In addition to all the militaristic rules and dicey personal boundaries, there was zero encouragement to be yourself. In fact, the total opposite was true. Yourself was an impediment to productivity. Yourself was under strict orders to stay at home under the stairs. (A bit like Sissy Spacek in the movie *Carrie*.)

Today's workplace is kinder, gentler, and infinitely less Orwellian. There are, however, mysterious cultural shifts and innovations that have added complexity to the whole process of getting, keeping, and enjoying a job. Can you speak kombucha?

How to Write a Résumé

Résumés tend to be very standard. Applicants use the same boring formats that they swipe off the Internet. All hail, the cover letter! The cover letter, rather than the résumé itself, is your big opportunity to make an impression. But I would encourage you not to use your cover letter as an avenue for self-expression but to be more cunning and strategic instead.

Most applicants today focus too much on heralding their otherworldly magnificence. Everyone entering today's job market is packaging themselves as a shimmering paragon. Newsflash: it's boring. Employees don't really care that you worked in a leper colony on weekends, nor do they believe you.

You must dial back the me, me, me self-congratulatory tone.

Instead of blowing your own trumpet, you are better served to kvell about the fabulosity of the organization you are hoping to join. Display an encyclopedic knowledge of the company's achievements, underscoring what has attracted you. Instead of "hire me because I'm so great," it should be more "here's why I think your company is so great and why I would kill to be part of it." This earnest enthusiastic approach involves more work. You must exercise due diligence on prospective employers and customize your cover letters accordingly. Your nerdy enthusiasm will make you a total standout from all the other chest-beating applicants, and your efforts will help you get your hoof in the door.

Speaking of hooves in doors, this is the perfect juncture to confront that contemporary scourge: nepotism. Full disclosure: when I was sixteen, I was the beneficiary of nepotism. Betty Doonan pulled some strings and got me a job at the bottle-top factory, down by the river. When young people ask me how I got my start, I tell them this (true) story, and they stare at me in disbelief.

Work has indeed been my best beauty treatment. I believe in hard work. It keeps the wrinkles out of the mind and the spirit.

— Helena Rubinstein

Here is the good news: while nepotism is still rife, employers are becoming increasingly uncomfortable with the idea of only hiring privileged, connected kids. As a result, they are actively seeking worthy individuals from bottle-top factory bumfuck. Being utterly devoid of connections now carries its own brand of chic, but only if you shriek it from the rooftops, by which I mean, be sure to mention it in that blessed cover letter. Bluntly declare that you have no connections, family or otherwise, and that you are from Nowheresville, USA. By doing so, you are throwing down the gauntlet and daring the potential employer to look beyond the sons and daughters of celebrity and privilege, and at you.

If that doesn't work, you could try exaggerating your "connections" for comic effect. Example: my grandmother once appeared on *Match Game* and won $1,700, or my uncle is a dog groomer who volunteers at a shelter and once clipped a dog that was later adopted by David Hasselhoff.

A jaunty chapeau will make you memorable.

How to Interview

In the old days, a job interview was more like an espionage interrogation. The interviewer would ask a couple of questions—what are your strengths? Why did you get fired from your last job?—and then remain mute while you, the interviewee, babbled extemporaneously and sweated profusely. In other words, the employer/interviewer had all the power. My husband claims that our first date ran exactly along these lines. I sat mute like a stuffed gerbil while he filled the awkward silence with anxious jabbering and bubbly anecdotes.

During my early years at Barneys, I was, unsurprisingly, an expert at the say-nothing-and-let-the-other-person-do-all-the-talking hiring technique. I would ask a question and then stare unblinkingly at the prospective employee as if we were cast adrift in an Antonioni movie. The poor victim would talk and talk and talk, anxiously filling the void, unaware that he/she/they was revealing key facets of their work history, aptitudes, and insanity level.

Worry not. You will no longer be subjected to this interview technique. Now everything has reversed. The interviewer feels a crushing burden to sell the opportunity to the future employee. You will be lucky if you can get a word in edgewise. This is where you, drawing on all that diligence, lob a few insightful questions of your own. The interviewer will be relieved to ditch the sales pitch and connect on a substantive level.

How to Be Yourself in a Workplace Utopia

The old notion of enduring a boring job in order to pay your bills now seems like a Dickensian trope. All that tyrannical oversight is being replaced by vegan cupcakes, standing desks, nap rooms, and complimentary kombucha on tap. Employees today are not only pampered, they are treated like fragile, temperamental child-pageant contestants, perpetually on the verge of becoming offended, anxious,

Enjoying "me time" under the printer.

or indignant—or allergic to wheat and cilantro. Meditation rooms abound. Wellness and mindfulness are the new workplace priorities.

Tread cautiously into this new utopia. As sensitive and "caring" as the new workplace is, I fear that—and this is a megaparadox—it might fall short in tolerating feisty individuality. There is still, nevertheless, a culture of conformity. Dissent is unwelcome. Not sure what I am referring to? Try chewing on a stick of beef jerky on Tofu Tuesdays and get back to me. Try wearing sequined stilettos when everyone else is wearing Allbirds. Clearly, it's not hard to stand out in this sea of namaste. If you are a cynic with a rebellious streak, you may find yourself being dragged off to HR for yet another round of sensitivity training.

How to Keep Your Job While Remaining Yourself
Your challenges go way beyond learning how to comport yourself on Wheat-Free Wednesdays. Here's the deal: you did such a fantastic job of standing out and asking informed, nerdy questions at your interview that you have already acquired something of a reputation. In fact, you are the new bright hope, a mini-Messiah. This is not a good thing. Burdened by high expectations, you must take care not to blunder about, lest you expose your flaws. How do you make sure you don't fall short and get fired? You need to come up

with a radical strategy: show up ten minutes early and leave ten minutes late.

Old-fashioned punctuality has untold benefits, especially in this brave new world. That extra time will allow you to masticate your locally harvested granola in peace and then reapply your lip gloss. You will have a moment to formulate your thoughts for that upcoming meeting. In an era when employees are loosey-goosey about timekeeping—Heather just texted from her reiki session and she's running behind—the punctuality habit will mark you as an enigma, a strange combo of reliable and unknowable. Nobody will quite know what to make of you. Colleagues will project all kinds of stuff onto you. You, meanwhile, will be craftily learning the ropes.

How to Avoid Becoming a Much Larger Self

Your biggest challenge upon entering a new workplace is to avoid the cruelty-free kale chips! Massive complimentary snack centers the size of convenience stores have erupted in every working environment, with dire consequences. Young employees have barely shed their "freshman fifteen" before they start packing on their "Facebook fifteen." Introducing this kind of calorific temptation into the lives of young people whose jobs are sedentary is nothing short of sadistic.

There is a solution: petition to have the snack center removed. Caution. This may well elicit a wave of rage from colleagues. If the debate starts to get testy, introduce a little levity: suggest that HR provide free shock-collars that are triggered whenever employees come within three feet of the dried non-GMO cranberries.

How to Look Like Yourself at Work

Sartorial informality in the workplace is a done deal. Don't try to fight it. Instead, be glad that your colleagues have surrendered to all those Zuckerbergian slate gray T-shirts and hoodies. The landscape is ready and waiting for you and your self-expression, and, more specifically, your chosen

When faced with sexism or ageism or lookism...ask yourself the following question: "Is this person in between me and what I want to do?" If the answer is no, ignore it and move on.

— Tina Fey

signature flourish. (See the "Style" chapter.) Whether you are sitting at your desk or video-conferencing from home, your main focus of attention should be above the waist, or maybe even above the neck.

Dos and Don'ts

— **DO** remember that making an effort with your appearance—especially if you are on a group conference chat and still wearing PJ bottoms—is a form of good manners.

— **DO** add a color tint to your reading glasses. Tip: Blue tints look glam in brown/tortoiseshell frames. Black frames scream for warm apricot tints, even yellow, if you are an edgy chick.

— **DO** explore the world of '80s hair accessories. Remember the oversized silk scrunchie and the topsy tail? Why not spearhead a one-woman revival? Is it too soon to bring back barrettes and velvet Hillary headbands? There's only one way to find out. Be mindful of not offending older colleagues who are still rocking their '80s banana clips from the first time around.

— **DON'T** steal somebody else's schtick. If Maureen in shipping is the acknowledged earring queen, then don't start competing by overloading your lobes. Find your own lane.

— **DON'T** jeopardize your credibility. If you are a medical professional or your job involves handling vast sums of (other people's) money, then you should avoid excessive flamboyance, or any flamboyance at all. Why? A sequined jumpsuit with a matching purse and turban can torpedo your gravitas and erode your credibility. (And that's just the men.) Sometimes those gray basics and beige essentials are a better choice.

Finally, and most importantly, by upping the style ante, you enhance the lives of your colleagues. I'm deadly serious.

How to Sit on a Buckwheat Pillow

First came those bouncy balls, featured on *Portlandia*.
Then came standing and treadmill desks. I applauded these
innovations, but assumed that the expense—nonessential
at best—should be covered by the employee. I have since had
a change of heart: Given the lethal potential of the snack
centers detailed above, I wonder if these dynamic desks
should not be provided gratis. Or how about as a reward for
productivity—yes, Hermione, you may have a treadmill desk,
but only if your team meets this quarter's sales goals.

How to Sit on Your Emotions

Formerly unheard of in the workplace, weeping is now
ubiquitous. While I am all for colleagues being more
expressive, I cannot help but wonder if weeping, once it has
become normalized, qualifies as meaningful self-expression.
If everyone is doing it, what can it possibly signify?

Throughout history, crying has gone in and out of
fashion. In eighteenth-century France, aristocratic men
would diffuse conflict by turning on the waterworks, hence
those giant lacey mouchoirs, which they kept jammed up
their sleeves.

My non-aristo Irish grandpa was a tough old dude who
only wore his teeth for funerals and gambled on horses.
If my sister or I would cry, Grandpa would ask the following
question: "Is your bladder near your eyeballs?" When he saw
that I was going to be a short kid, dollar signs rolled in his
eyes. He exhorted Betty Doonan to put "a wee drop of gin"
in my milk to further stunt my growth so that I might become
a jockey, thereby bringing some much-needed additional cash
into the house. When I passed the jockey height, he looked
like he might actually cry.

I have inherited Grandpa's unsympathetic attitudes,
including an aversion to crying in the workplace. Surely
you can be yourself at work without being emotionally
incontinent? You can also be sad or mad without crying.

The main reason not to cry at work is that weeping is, frankly speaking, not a good look. Most people appear and sound grotesque when they cry. Their faces turn into a kabuki mask of grimacing agony, and they make appalling noises. Very few individuals are "pretty criers." The tears glide down their flawless faces in a choreographed flow—like Catherine Deneuve in *The Umbrellas of Cherbourg*. No wailing. No keening. As a self-confessed ugly crier, I am very jealous of them.

Another reason not to cry at work—brace yourself for a little mansplaining—is that it rekindles all kinds of uncomfortable stereotypes about female "hysteria" and "the weaker sex." Did Amelia Earhart cry at work? I doubt it. #feminism

There is one massive benefit for employees of all genders to stifling tears: you will retain a nuclear weapon in your arsenal. Keep the weeping in reserve, and when something truly terrible happens, your tears will signify the depth of your reaction. Think of that moment when, after half a century of stoicism, your dad finally cries, and it blows your mind.

How to Be Yourself at Office Occasions

AT A TEAM-BUILDING EVENT
Team-building events are like reality television shows: the people who succeed and hang on longest are the ones who keep mum, and observe, observe, observe. How might you be yourself at a team-building event? Don't. Leave yourself under the stairs with Carrie, or stuff him/her/them into the hotel minibar. These group encounters are a great opportunity to go into espionage mode.

Follow this advice, and I guarantee that you will come away with masses of strategic ideas that will lead to success and promotion. If, instead, you spend the whole weekend trying to make a big fat impression on the group, all you will come away with is a hangover.

Team-building events require a suspension of cynicism.

ON YOUR BIRTHDAY

I recently walked into a Midtown corporate office and heard a terrifying noise. It sounded like a rabid baboon was attacking a flock of seagulls. As I passed the glass-paneled office, I saw the source of the racket: In the center of the room stood a young lady. She was surrounded by ramparts of vegan cupcakes and caterwauling well-wishers. "Happy birthday!" they shrieked, oversized party balloons bobbing above their heads. iPhones snapped and Instas were instantly posted. The focus of the attention, the birthday girl herself, appeared paralyzed with anxiety amid all the streamers and balloons.

Don't let the birthday brigade mess with your head.

Simply put: the modern birthday has become little more than an excruciating hazing ritual.

Solution: When hired, explain to your HR exec that something ghastly happened to you—no need to specify—during a childhood birthday and that the mere sight of a party balloon triggers a crippling PTSD. Explain that, in lieu of the cupcake shriek-fest, you would prefer to spend an hour in one of the green-certified, gender-neutral wellness rooms, alone.

AT THE OFFICE PARTY

When I recall workplace parties from the late '60s and early '70s, my blood runs cold. All that repression referred to above was a ticking time bomb that would inevitably explode at the annual staff Christmas party. On this occasion, we drones were encouraged to "enjoy a little yuletide cheer." We did, turning what was supposed to be a wholesome mixer into Sodom and Gomorrah.

You will never encounter such excesses in today's workplace—tawdry behavior of any kind has become the ultimate crime. That does not mean that socializing today is any less fraught. Far from it. Your lovely colleagues—

The office parties of my youth were full of surprises.

remember, they spend all day texting and emailing, avoiding face-to-face communication—are, for the most part, ill-equipped to engage in frothy social banter.

Below is a basic tool kit, designed to address the challenges of any workplace party:

1. When conversation flags, pull out your phone and flaunt your poodle. Pets are the ultimate social WD-40. Even the most inhibited individuals become animated when talking about regal hounds and rescue mutts.
2. Cringing at the thought of making conversation with socially anxious colleagues who may or may not be pet owners? Appoint yourself the official server. Bypass the chitchat, grab a bottle, and whirl around the room topping off glasses. This puts you firmly in the driver's seat: you can underserve the braying bores and overserve the shy, demure types.
3. Truculent, inebriated revelers are rare but need to be dealt with forcefully. For bold solutions, I refer you

What I don't like about office Christmas parties is looking for a job the next day.

— Phyllis Diller

to the legendary society hostess Elsa Maxwell. When dealing with male drunks, she suggested that you "order the offender off the premises in no uncertain terms" and "be prepared to back up the order with a discreet show of bodily force." Regarding female drunks, she recommended the following: "Simply go up behind her and give her pearls a twist."

4. If you have any say in the event decor, try to introduce a seating/lounging area, even if it's a circle of cheapo beanbag chairs. If you have a big budget, then create a beanbag forest. (See the "People" chapter.)

5. Irish exits are the ultimate in good manners. Nothing casts a pall over an event quite like an entire roomful of people saying goodnight to each other, over and over. Sashay away, when nobody is watching.

How to Quit

Keep it simple: give plenty of notice and avoid any emotional shenanigans. You have managed to keep the waterworks under control up to this point. No need to turn them on now.

Do not, under any circumstance, schedule a meeting with a company head so that you can bore him/her/them to death with how grateful you are. Shut up...and head for the exit. Your dignified exit will leave a positive impression. At the very least people will say, "Yes, I liked Mildred. She made a dignified exit."

If they offer to throw you a going-away party, you must refuse. These are excruciating occasions—akin to those frightening birthday parties—when everyone stares at you while you clutch a paper cup full of moderately priced Chardonnay. Another reason not to have a party: the company may well make you a counteroffer. Keeping everyone in the boardroom for hours and taking sentimental selfies when you are going to end up back at work the following Monday is nothing short of psychotic.

If your boss actually does make you a counteroffer—we need you!—keep your emotional self under wraps. Respond that you, of course, need the weekend to think about it. And then run home, pull out the calculator, and figure out exactly how much extra dough it will take to get you to stay.

Save the explosive, creative, charismatic you for brainstorming meetings and the motivation of your underlings.

As you can see, basic workplace hiring/firing stuff is best handled with a cool head. Shove the full scope of your fantabulous self on the back burner and adopt a strategic, old-fashioned grown-up approach. Yes, if you follow my advice, thou shall have many, many underlings.

How to Be Yourself After Getting Fired

If you get fired, then try to get another job immediately. It might not be easy but see if you can find something that keeps you busy and pays your bills while you plot your next move. Early in her career, Amy Sedaris worked as a cocktail waitress. She regards it as time well spent: "I learned so much. I learned that it's better to say 'how 'bout a gin and tonic?'—rather than 'how 'bout another gin and tonic?' You can't make people feel like they are alcoholic even if they are. It makes them uneasy."

The philosopher Simone Weil elected to work in a car factory a couple of days a week, to clear her head and stay in touch with *les misérables*. I am a big proponent of getting your hands dirty. In my youth I had many factory jobs. I value this experience. The tedium taught me endurance and made me appreciate all my subsequent jobs. Even to this day, if I am struggling with a particular project, I think, "This job sucks, but it sure beats washing dishes while standing on a box at the Mars Bar factory staff canteen in Slough, in 1968."

When you reach out for another job, any employer with half a brain will be impressed by your spunky work ethic and your drive to take responsibility for your bills and for yourself. They may well be intrigued to hear about your experiences as a JFK baggage handler or how you fared when your only colleague was the trash compactor in the bowels of Chipotle.

Rough Trade: Working with Your Hands

If that trusty solar-powered kombucha machine went kaput, how many of your colleagues would know how to fix it? If that treadmill desk jammed, would anyone be able to figure out how to reattach the belt? Much contemporary employment does not require manual skills. How many of your colleagues can wield a toilet plunger with any degree of success?

I am a big believer in manual competence. I can declog gutters and toilets. I can change a car tire. I could probably figure out how to change the oil. My years of prop making, set building, and mannequin fluffing have given me a breezy, confident relationship with the physical world. Trades make people happy.

In my experience, trades are every bit as conducive to self-expression as more prestigious jobs. They are also a reliable source of income: landscape gardener, sushi chef, electrician, DJ, florist, and...drumroll... hairdresser. Learn to cut and/or color hair and you will work forever. No matter what horrors engulf an economy, people still pay to get

A trade = mad skills and major job satisfaction.

I've found that your chances for happiness are increased if you wind up doing something that is a reflection of what you loved most when you were somewhere between nine and eleven years old.

— Walter Murch

their hair done. You never spend time in a hair salon and think, "If only these poor unhappy people could work in a place where they get to be themselves and have fun." In the hair community, everyone is fully actualized.

My husband built a career based on his ceramic skills. He can make stuff, and, after twenty-five years in the design biz, his happiest moments still occur when he is putzing around and throwing clay in his pottery studio. After various waitressing jobs, my niece Tanya doffed her apron and successfully trained to become a yoga teacher. Her classes are now the talk of South London.

Writing is now my métier, but before I became a writer, my trade was, as noted above, window dresser. I spent my days schlepping mannequins and making giant poodles out of feather dusters. I feel so lucky to have stumbled into this fabulous milieu that I called home for four decades. In the window-display world, being yourself is a prerequisite.

When the US outsourced manufacturing to developing countries, we waved goodbye to many of these skill-based jobs. Don't let that deter you. If you have a skill—crochet, welding, electronics, macramé, doll making, weaving, making marionettes or miniature dog portraits—it is now possible to launch a small business. No, I am not talking about seeking financing and "making a killing." Instead, why not open an Etsy shop, thereby promoting and selling your crafty wares with minimal outlay and maximum creative satisfaction? No venture capital needed. Much of this book slags off the Internet and social media. Time to acknowledge that they can also be forces for good, a way to market your crafty, creative self. Maybe you won't make a ton of money. Maybe you will never be able to give up your day job. But you will have an outlet for self-expression. #priceless

How to Make It Werk
I got lucky. In 1985 I found Barneys, and Barneys found me. I went all in. Over the next thirty-five years, the job evolved

and expanded and was never not stimulating. So I stayed. Every now and then, I would have a what-if moment. What if I jumped ship? Then one glorious day, I met Susan Lucci. She played Erica Kane on *All My Children* from 1970 to 2011. We compared notes regarding our long-term employment: Lucci fixed me with those gorgeous brown eyes and declared, "When you have a great gig, you don't walk away. That would be insane."

Lucci and I surrendered. We allowed our jobs to define us, and we could not have been happier. The rewards were significant. (Ditto the awards. I have a shelf full, and Lucci has several rooms full.) But that was then and this is now. Do not, dear reader, attempt to replicate our journeys. Why? This model, the Lucci/Doonan surrender, is no longer applicable. It's very pre-Internet. It's very last century. The world was a smaller place back then.

Today's workplace is far more dynamic and, despite that gurgling feel-good stream of kombucha, more demanding and treacherous. Loyalty and surrender are no longer enough. The stakes are higher, as is the cost of living. The volatility is greater, as are the opportunities. You must take inventory of your aptitudes, idiosyncrasies, and skills, and figure out how best to use them, switching jobs whenever a viable option presents itself. If you wish to become successful, you must become your own ruthless Hollywood agent.

But what if you don't give a shit?

For those who are more focused on personal growth and less inclined to battle it out on this new overachieving, everyone-deserves-to-be-a-CEO career landscape, there is another equally valid path. Become a collage artist. Collage your career.

A collaged career has two principal thrusts: the bill-paying components and the non-bill-paying components. The former is self-explanatory. The latter thrust offers you unlimited crafty-ass self-expression and/or spiritual satisfaction. Example: You may wish to devote that non-bill-

Life is not a checklist of acquisition or achievement.
Your qualifications, your CV, are not your life, though you will meet many people of my age and older who confuse the two.

— J. K. Rowling

paying time to abstract expressionist oil painting or to an idealistic nonprofit venture, or both. Who knows? You may get lucky and, with the help of your crafty paws and that aforementioned Etsy shop, turn a creative outlet into a bill-paying moneymaker.

Final nugget: Chances are that you will spend approximately ninety thousand hours at work, so it behooves you to make your days bearable. This may or may not involve becoming rich and successful. Power and shekels are no guarantee of personal satisfaction. As you attempt to claw your way to the top, do not lose sight of your psychological needs. Make choices that bring you satisfaction and joy.

I have met many people who ascended to the top of the heap, only to become irate and remote. I myself clawed my way to the middle, and when I realized how happy I was, I stopped clawing and stayed exactly where I was. When I glanced up through the glass ceiling, I saw stress and unwieldy responsibility. I realized that I had no desire to become CEO of Barneys—as creative director I was having way too much fun.

If being top dog makes you happy, then have at it. Live your truth. For everyone else I say this: be wary of jeopardizing your peace of mind in the pursuit of status, money, or power. Needlepoint that!

DECOR

Artist Duncan Grant invented bohemian funk decor.

There is an intriguing new presence in your workplace. Let's call her Angie. Angie combines the modish hauteur of Bella Hadid with the appealing self-deprecation of Phoebe Waller-Bridge. Her silky hair is scraped into a ponytail. Eyeliner is applied with precision while she drinks a Diet Fresca and checks her emails. Her lightly battered black vintage Chanel suit is worn above the knee, paired with poison-green wellies. Her purse is made from scraps of metallic leather that she found in a trash bag on Thirty-Ninth Street. She made it herself! Angie is jagged with sophistication but also hilarious and down to earth.

Angie's effortless panache is reflected in her manner, her appearance, and her work. She has clearly figured it all out. If anybody is living her truth, it's Angie. You want her to be your friend, but you just assume, based on her general air of having it all, that she has no need to add the likes of you to her trendy claque.

One day you are walking down the street, and you bump into Angie. She is struggling with a bunch of shopping bags.

You offer to give her a hand. She accepts. You are happy to play handmaiden to Angie. Having never been to Angie's home, you are excited to get a peek. Angie's creative charisma must surely have manifested itself in a stunning decor. You wonder if you can score a few selfies with Angie, in her residence. As you enter the lobby of her apartment building, she tells her doorman, "This is my friend from work." Angie just called you her friend!

Funny how things can turn so nasty, so quickly. Before Angie has even had time to take off her coat and offer you a glass of water, you are wishing that you had never been born.

To say you are disgusted with Angie's living conditions would be an understatement. No, Angie is not some psycho hoarder. If only her apartment was that interesting. It's worse than that. Neither chic nor shabby, it's just plain naff. There is nothing fun or idiosyncratic about it. There is nothing Angie about it.

Angie seems neither proud nor ashamed of her home. She makes no excuses. As you stare at the beige/greige bamboo-print, seen-better-days wallpaper and jade-green synthetic velvet drapes trimmed with rose-pink dingle-ball fringe, you wait for her to explain that this is just the apartment of a (very) depressed aunt who has let her stay for a couple of weeks. Or that she rented the place furnished and is about to give it a wrecking ball do over. But she doesn't. Angie tells you, instead, that she has lived here since leaving college and proffers a bowl of dusty jellybeans.

Not giving a toss about your decor is a crime against humanity, a missed opportunity for you, and a potential source of PTSD for others.

You cannot get out of there quickly enough. The dissonance between Angie's place and the mythological Angie is

terrifying, begging the question: Who is the real Angie?
Is she the inspiring, stylish colleague? Or is she the depressive
weirdo who collects chipped Hummel figurines and sits on
chintzy French Provençal furniture that was purchased,
presumably by her parents, when the original *Dynasty* aired?

The Angie syndrome is not uncommon. We Brit gays used
to call it "all fur coat and no knickers." Meaning, a fab facade
and no backup. I vividly recall, back in the freewheeling '70s,
meeting some swashbuckling hottie at a disco and thinking,
"Wow! What a happening dude!" Then you get back to Mr.
Hottie's pad and spot the depressing café curtains framing
the kitchen serving hatch and the beige Naugahyde recliner
with the cigarette burns, and you immediately contemplate
hanging yourself from those café curtains.

Vivienne Westwood once said, "You have a more interesting
life if you wear impressive clothes." The same could be said of
decor. Impressive idiosyncratic decor—decor that expresses
you—can improve your life. How? Decor is a creative outlet,
but it also offers you a therapeutic opportunity to build a
concrete 3-D roadmap to your identity. *You want to know who
I am? Just look around.* Decor allows you to clarify and confirm
your understanding of yourself while communicating the best
aspects of that self to others.

The truth is that anyone can acquire an impressive decor.
Just as with impressive clothing, money is not the deciding
factor. Often the less money you spend, the more successful
the decor. (I once created baronial splendor by glue-gunning
thrift-store velvet drapes to the walls, ceiling, and windows
of a South London crash pad.) There are no pass/fails when
it comes to decor. The only crime is nondecor, an Angie-style
failure to utilize self-expression in your home. If not *chez toi*,
then where?

Tribes and Tribulations

The best way to develop a connection between your personal
style and your pad—thereby avoiding an Angie debacle—is to

Birds are so much wiser than we. A robin builds a nest for robins. A seagull builds a nest for seagulls. They don't copy each other or build themselves nests as described in the *Birds Decorating Magazine*.

— Dorothy Draper

study people who have done just that. These decor-achievers fall into specific tribes. Join the tribe that most vigorously jiggles your drapes and tassels. If no tribe resonates with you, feel free to start your own.

The Artist in Residence

When I walk into Sephora, I always take note of those blokes behind the counter who wear lots of mascara and foundation—far more than the average female customer—and I think, "Yes, I understand it. You are surrounded by makeup all day long. It's only a matter of time before you start slapping it on your own face." And so it is with artists. They toil in their studios all day long with all variety of materials. It is inevitable that their creativity starts to bust through the confines of the studios and into their homes.

Bloomsbury bisexual Duncan Grant applied his art to murals, carpets, and, most famously, the painted fireplace at Charleston, the farmhouse where, in the early twentieth century, he lived a life of bohemian free-loving self-expression. (No, not just in the fireplace, everywhere in the house.)

Artists who create shocking work create shocking interiors. They attack their homes with no preconceived ideas and total creative abandon. Cary Leibowitz, the perverse and enigmatic artist also known as Candy Ass, smothers his walls with jarring vintage wallpapers and the works of other artists, creating a totally proprietorial look every bit as bizarre as he is—and I say that with love.

Sculptor and jeweler Andrew Logan—the creator and host of the Alternative Miss World contest—encrusts his walls, furniture, and light fixtures with broken mirrors and jewels, turning his pad into a giant billboard for his fantastical jewelry. In a similar vein, we have the late, great Tony Duquette. He took found objects and gilded and elevated them into palatial adornments, turning his homes into demented and fabulous Hollywood sets. He was a genius, but not at installing sprinkler systems. Two of his

Tony Duquette unfurled his creative id *chez lui*.

masterpiece residences were destroyed by fire. I once asked him if he would collaborate with me on an installation at Barneys: "Yes, on one condition: you must flood the main floor of your store and fill it with water lilies." I have often wondered if this was an attempt at fire safety.

The Ancien Régime

Madame de Pompadour, the mistress of Louis XV, was the first posh lady to obsess about her interiors. (There might have been others before her, but Pompadour obviously had a better publicist because she is the one we all remember.) If you think Versailles is a bit over the top, blame Mme de Pompadour. She filled the place with billowing drapes, paintings by François Boucher, gilded boiserie, and porcelain from the Sèvres factory, which she owned. The Pompadour tradition was carried right through into the last century by heiresses such as Doris Duke, C. Z. Guest, and Gloria

Vanderbilt, who, by the way, also wore caftans that matched her drapes.

Today, there is no shortage of rich, posh ladies, but many have abandoned baroque embellishments in favor of starchitect-designed spaces garnished with minimal furniture and works by prestige investment artists such as Damien Hirst, Jeff Koons, and Kehinde Wiley. Thankfully, there are still some individuals—the Queen of England, Susan Gutfreund, Tory Burch, Liz Lange—who are kicking it old school, sleeping in four-poster beds with tented ceilings and dreaming of the richesse of Pompadour. Ralph Lauren is an honorary member of this posh-lady group.

Before you pull out the pitchforks and join an anarchist group, take a moment to consider the issue of job creation. These posh ladies are, and have always been, the patron saints of drapery and soft furnishings. Every time a poodle pees on a chaise longue, it is sent out for reupholstery. (The couch, not the poodle.)

Their reverence for history and tradition and glamour has sustained an entire skill-based industry of makers and craftsman, just as it did when Madame de Pompadour was alive.

Many of the collaborating decorators of this genre—Mario Buatta, Albert Hadley, Sister Parish, Renzo Mongiardino, and Dorothy Draper—are deceased. However, there is a new wave of enablers—Miles Redd,

Pompadour adored pomp. *Pourquoi pas?*

Celerie Kemble, Alexa Hampton, Mark D. Sikes—who are helping posh ladies keep their inner Pompadour in full bloom.

The Heritage Hipsters

They try as hard as possible not to appear posh. They work in Brooklyn microbreweries, and all they want for Christmas is a crate of the Beekman Boys' artisanal goat-milk soap or to swim in a vat of molten Mast Brothers chocolate. At holiday time, they gift each other organic axes. They love reclaimed wood and anything that has been salvaged or repurposed, including ancient factory tables, federal office furniture circa 1940, and rusting Ford pickups. They celebrate the earthy, pioneering aesthetic. *Butch* is the word that springs to mind,

Heritage hipsters are intoxicated by rusticity.

though they would never use it for fear of sounding not butch. Their favorite words are *authentic* and *honest* and *fair trade*. Even though they have never been hunting, they love taxidermy. They also love ink, plaid shirts, facial hair —and that's just the women. No, but seriously, heritage hipster style is relentlessly masculine, albeit of the nontoxic variety.

The less extreme version of this style—and the real indicator of its spreading popularity—is represented by shiplap lovers Chip and Joanna Gaines, who have feminized the hip/heritage style of decorating—*Dieu merci!*—and made it more accessible to the masses.

The Erotic Exquisites

There is a long tradition of strippers, soubrettes, and burlesque queens living in satin-upholstered jewelry boxes. The concept of the *poule de luxe*, the *grande horizontale*, the kept

A house is like a portrait, and, in the end, the place has to look like the person living in it.

— India Mahdavi

woman—see Émile Zola's *Nana*—ruthlessly bankrupting her benefactor with demands for silk drapes and crystal chandeliers for her boudoir is a tale as old as lingerie. As I consider this tribe, the names of famous burlesque queens— Bettie Page, Gypsy Rose Lee, Lili St. Cyr, Blaze Starr—whirl through my mind like twirling pasties.

The slinky aesthetic includes black lacquer, pink satin, leopard print. Remember the incredible Bobby Trendy, who created satin and marabou boudoirs for the late Anna Nicole Smith?

Pearl and Earl Harbour surrounded by glamorous eclectica.

The chic-de-la-chic couture version of this decor tribe is epitomized by the incredible Dita Von Teese, whose meticulous artistry and sense of style is reflected in her home and has elevated all aspects of the burlesque aesthetic. Dita celebrates the artificial glamour of the golden age of Hollywood—when fresh-faced Norma Jeanes were transformed into heart-stopping Marilyns—and uses it as inspiration for her appearance and her glam decor, a sensual retreat where custom murals and silver leaf provide the backdrop for taxidermy, Hollywood memorabilia, and fetish art.

In a category all her own, we have the magnificent Pearl Harbour. The one-time North Beach stripper straddled the zeitgeist of late twentieth-century culture, dancing on stage with the Tubes, marrying Paul Simonon from the Clash, and then becoming a committed rocker. Pearl's Hollywood pad is a perfect reflection of her incredible past: elements of punk, rock and roll, and burlesque—her collection of original burlesque posters is world class—overlap just as they have in Pearl's novelistic life. Pearl says, "Home decor is so important to me because a festive, over-the-top home encourages me to keep a sense of humor about myself, and it helps me when I'm getting dressed for the day…. I can overaccessorize and blend in with my surroundings!"

The Mod Squad

The optimism of the postwar era gave us the midcentury aesthetic, epitomized by Verner Panton, Charles and Ray Eames, and Alexander Girard. Graphic, geometric, futuristic, and playful, the mod aesthetic is addictive, hip but instantly recognizable. This can take a bite out of your self-expression factor. If you cram your pad full of Eames chairs and Eames this and that, it's going to end up saying more about Charles and Ray than it does about you.

Lisa Perry, fashion designer and pop/mod connoisseur, has successfully infused the mod aesthetic with her own sensibility by introducing elements of surprise and humor.

I believe that everything in one's house should be comfortable, but one's bedroom must be more than comfortable: it must be intimate, personal, one's secret garden, so to speak. It may be as simple as a convent cell and still have this quality of the personality of its occupant.

— Elsie de Wolfe

In Lisa's words: "I was always a bit turned off by the term mod. I felt it conjured up an image of Lulu in *To Sir with Love* or Courrèges models in head-to-toe silver paillettes and white go-go boots. Not that I didn't love all of that! But at some point, for it to be relevant and not look too retro, mod had to become modern. That's what I try to do in fashion and in home design. It's all about the vintage and new mix. Any head-to-toe retro look or one-note home design can become costumey or boring. But a large neon-orange Cesar boob in the middle of an all white room or a giant Robert Indiana tapestry in a serene setting will add just the right kind of pop! The end goal for me is to put a smile on someone's face."

Verner Panton lived inside a lava lamp.

The Dolly Birds

Johnny Depp is drowning in Barbie dolls. Demi Moore has an exquisite collection of realistic artist-created babies. Celebrities love to decorate their houses with dolls. Why not? If you are a performer, I am sure it's nice to have an audience, a phalanx of acolytes, welcoming you home with unblinking eyes. But what do these collections say about the psyches of the collectors? Are they bonkers? Or is the doll obsession a therapeutic one?

Barbra Streisand has not only ramparts of dolls in her Malibu retreat, but also a storage facility in her basement designed to look like quaint shops selling dolly clothing.

She attributes this impulse to dolly deprivation, a compensation for the childhood years of austerity when she had no dolls.

Fashion designer Anna Sui's apartment is filled with massive collections of curated flea market and eBay finds, which include Navajo dolls and creations designed by

Marilyn Neuhart for Alexander Girard. Of the origins of her ever-growing collection, Anna offers the following insight: "I remember seeing Marilyn Neuhart dolls in the pages of *Seventeen* magazine when they showed cute bedroom ideas, usually

Marilyn Neuhart enjoying her doll installation.

one doll per boudoir. But of course, me being me, I now own a mountain of them!"

The perimeter of writer Lynn Yaeger's Greenwich Village aerie is lined with deeply distressed Victorian monkeys and fraying rag dolls, orphans of long-vanished toy chests. For Lynn, these signify valiant survival: "Who says you have to be perfect to be loved? They're old and worn—but they're still cute!" The charm of these relics has clearly informed Lynn's legendary fashion look: "I guess faded flapper boudoir doll could sort of describe my style."

In my own homes, the tables are always set, even if I'm not expecting guests. If I want to get rid of somebody, the settings have a practical purpose... they'll look at the table and comment that I must be having guests—perhaps they'd better leave.

— Liberace

Bejeweled in his bubble bath, the late, great Liberace.

The Emperors of Camp

What do Russian oligarchs, Donald Trump, and Liberace have in common? They are all very camp. The desire to live like King Solomon or a spendaholic Roman emperor is the very definition of camp. Camp is a lethal combo of artifice, theatricality, and exaggeration, which describes the hairdos of both Trump and Lib. The two men share a nonironic obsession with adornment and prestige, matched by an indifference to notions of good taste.

Fun fact: Several years ago, I ran into an individual who was dropping off frocks at Trump Tower. "Is it as hilarious as it looks in photos? What's it like?" My friend underscored the unintentional hilarity of the Greco-Roman Vegas casino decor. He explained that the overriding takeaway could be summed up in one word: *chlorine*. There are so many fountains and water features—all chlorinated to inhibit algae growth—that the place smells like a swimming pool. Now that is camp.

The Unclassifiables

Certain individuals are so highly idiosyncratic that their personal expression—what comes out when they pour their eccentricity into the interiors of their homes—does not align with any existing tribe. This is a good thing. Phyllis Diller's wig room falls into this category. Fright wigs were part of the Diller persona. To see them used as decor chez Diller makes perfect sense and creates a mise-en-scène that is both appalling and gorgeous at the same time.

Soccer legend Gigi Meroni enjoyed some success before being hit by a car. (The guy who ran him over went on to manage Gigi's soccer team.) During his heyday, the enigmatic Gigi—he also designed clothing and painted in oils—created a singular living space that appears to follow

Unwittingly avant-garde: Gigi Meroni and his electric heater.

I have Margaret Keane's paintings, which I love, hanging in my bedroom and dressing room, and I think I would start putting them in the bathrooms if the walls weren't tiled to the ceilings.

— Joan Crawford

no known aesthetic rules and gives mysterious prominence to a persimmon-hued electric heater. The results are far more intriguing than any high-priced "avant-garde" interior created today. Gigi has a lesson for all of us: you do you, and half a century later people will still be intrigued.

Now that you have encountered the various tribes—feeling a teensy bit like Margaret Mead?—it is time to figure out where you belong, especially if, like Angie, you have dropped the ball completely and are living in a dusty hole of naffness. Don't delay. Pick a tribe and begin to experiment. Do not be intimidated. For your convenience, the remainder of this chapter contains some easy solutions with maximal impact that are applicable to all tribes.

What was that? You want to know which tribe I belong to? I am a special case. I live with my interior decorator and benefit from his wisdom every day. Now it's your turn. Read on.

If you lived with Adele, would you go ask a stranger for singing lessons? If Albert Einstein were your roommate, would you go to evening classes to study the laws of physics? If you were married to Jonathan Adler for over two decades, would you attempt to write about the relationship between decor and personal expression without tapping into his vast trove of knowledge? #no *Et voilà!* A global exclusive: my first-ever interview with my husbear, designer and interior decorator Jonathan Adler.

SD: As you know, I have no sense of occasion, so I cannot remember when we met. Help me out. It was the mid-'90s, right?

JA: Totes. I was a clay-spattered potter—I was selling my pots at Todd Oldham's store and at Barneys—and you were a glam retail exec in a suit, known for his wacky window displays. We were set up on a blind date. I sweated a lot, but that was because I had rollerbladed to the date, and it was the middle of summer. I was twenty-eight. You were forty-two. Shocking, right?

My significant other decorated our living room while I cheered from the sidelines.

SD: At that point you were a long way from becoming an interior design czar, no offense.

JA: True. But I was always interested in interiors and how people might use their decor to express their most fabulous selves. When I was a kid, growing up in southern New Jersey, our house was a perfect expression of my parents' personalities: Marimekko shades, Danish mod furniture, and bursts of color. The vibe was optimistic '60s pop but also crafty. Our neighbor, Mrs. Goldstein, was a glamorous eccentric. She had a more flamboyant house with Lucite chairs and mod light fixtures. She wallpapered her kitchen with *New Yorker* covers. She embellished the various doors in her house with nails and wire. It was crafty but also swanky, and totally unpretentious. I grew up thinking that decor should be very personal. This is the key: there was no part of Mrs. Goldstein's house that did not scream "Mrs. Goldstein!"

SD: So let's say one is bored with one's pad but is too inert to undertake a major redo. In addition to Mrs. Goldstein's *New Yorker* wallpaper, give me some quick decor fixes.

JA: Start with a new light fixture. If you have some cash, then buy one of mine. If not, then make one. I'm serious. My mom did this when I was a kid. It was a sphere, white and architectural, made with white Styrofoam cups and a glue gun. It was very Courrèges. It's all a matter of taste. If you fancy a Victorian chandelier, then go for it. The key is to make a personal style statement that makes you feel good. Your home should be like a dose of Zoloft.

SD: You are the Oscar Wilde of decor. Very quotable. I have dredged up some ancient quotes of yours. I am going to fling them at you and see if you still stand by them. You once said, "Minimalism is a bummer." Still true?

JA: I have always been a maximalist. I equate minimalism with melancholy. Conversely, I equate flamboyant decor with positivity. Mies van der Rohe's philosophy was "Less is more." Mine is "Life's too short for minimalism." In fact, I think minimalism should be renamed miserable-ism. The real reason I recoil from minimalism is that it feels like an absence of personal expression. For some people minimalism connotes calm and serenity. I respect that, sort of.

SD: Another is "Handcrafted tchotchkes are life enhancing."

JA: I have always been a craftsperson. I have kept my Wallabees firmly planted in the craft world, right next to my pottery wheel. And when I design anything—a hotel, a restaurant, a rock star's pad—I always introduce handcrafted elements, handmade ceramic tiles, Peruvian wovens, sculpture, murals, etc. Handcrafted stuff allows for personal expression and creates a human connection. Got a blank wall? Then buy

a bunch of vintage macramé owls on Etsy and cover it!
Or learn to macramé and make them yourself.

SD: There are very few blank walls in our house. Let's talk about that.

JA: Blank walls are opportunities to make personal statements. An uptown shopaholic girl I know just created a fantastic art installation on a blank wall in her pad using vintage shopping bags from iconic stores. I give it a total thumbs up because it perfectly expresses her style. Our bathroom in our beach house had a large blank wall, and we hired a muralist to paint the word MISHEGAS in giant letters. This reflects my love of Yiddish and the fabulous chaos of our life in NYC.

SD: "Colors can't clash." Do you still stand by this statement?

JA: Color is very personal—one person's acid yellow is another person's beige. If you are a little reticent about color, it helps to create a more solid backdrop—chocolate brown or battleship gray—but then you can go crazy layering with mauve and fuchsia and red and beige! Yes, you heard right. Beige and pink look great together.

SD: You once said, "Put flowers in an umbrella stand and ostrich feathers in a candleholder." Were you having a Liberace moment?

JA: Repurposing objects allows for loads of self-expression. In the '60s, there was a trend for turning Victorian hip baths into armchairs. Holly Golightly's sparse decor consisted of an old enamel bathtub with the side sawn off—her couch!—and a packing crate which served as a coffee table. Dying!

SD: A scary one is "Clowns are creepy, but that doesn't mean you shouldn't put one over your fireplace." Really?

JA: Clowns are appalling and sinister and not for everyone. You need to be a confident decorator. I am something of a clown connoisseur. I like to think I am capable of weeding out the really naff ones.

SD: Back to color again. You once declaimed, "If I were a doctor I would prescribe yellow to cure all ills."

JA: I think I was a little off my meds that day, but I still dig yellow. Maybe you don't want to paint the entire room, but there are so many clever ways to introduce yellow into your life: Throw a bag of lemons into a giant shell. Put a yellow daisy in a bud vase or a beer bottle. Take that old Andy

Paint your pad with pillows. #selfexpression

Warhol *Velvet Underground & Nico* record album—the one with the banana on the cover—frame it and hang it over the toilet.

SD: You once said you believe that "tassels are the earrings of the home." Were you gargling with bong water that day?

JA: This interview is turning into the Spanish Inquisition, but I'm loving it. Whether they are discreet or baroque, I 100 percent stand by all tassels, forever. They look great dangling from door handles, light switches, window blinds, and, of course, your earlobes.

SD: You often talk about the concept of "insta-architecture." Explain.

JA: Renovations are insanely stressful. There are shortcuts to creating change with screens, curtains, and room dividers. String drapes and ball-chain curtains can create

Pick the blooms that tingle your chakras.

privacy without blocking light. And the vibe is supergroovy. The string drapes are very Big Sur, and the ball chains remind me of the old Four Seasons restaurant in NYC. Very *Mad Men*.

SD: Your first foray outside of pottery was into the world of pillows. Discuss this evolution.

JA: Two decades ago, I was down in Peru toiling at a workshop, and I met this fabulous chick named Charo, who was connected with all the local weavers. I asked her to weave some simple geometric designs in wool and alpaca. These early pillows are still in my collection today. For years, one of them sat on the set of *Will and Grace*. Pillows are the exclamation point of the home!

SD: *Tablescapes*? Did you invent that word?

JA: The late great Sir David Hicks invented *tablescapes*. They are a magnificent outlet for individualism and self-expression. You take all your favorite collections—seashells, crystals, paperweights, champagne corks, and memorabilia—and arrange them on a coffee table. Then rearrange and add more stuff—edit and rearrange.

SD: I met a lady who put mirrors on her fridge to minimize snacking. Thoughts?

JA: I am an enthusiastic snacker who needs to fight the impulse, so I like the idea of catching sight of myself lurching toward the fridge and then doing a guilty about-turn. This is a great example of tailoring your decor to meet personal needs. Mirrors are best used in recesses. By working with your architecture, you can really create depth. Leaning mirrors also add dimension. Don't go overboard, or you will end up with a disco, and not in a good way.

SD: What is the most inexpensive way to perk up your domain?

JA: I am big on flowers. For me, bold is better. Gladioli, daisies as previously stated, and, of course, sunflowers. Tulips, especially the strange purple and black ones. Lilies—fragrant, graphic, provocative—remind me of the fabulous Mrs. Goldstein, back in New Jersey.

SD: Big vases or small? You once said, "Bud vases are to flowers as hamburger helper is to ground beef."

JA: I think I might retract that statement, solely on the basis that it's a bit gross. Flowers and vases are a matter of personal taste. For a bohemian Brooklyn chick—she's probably reading Sylvia Plath—a few carefully chosen weeds in an old beer bottle can work fantastically.

SD: Thanks for the quips. Now get back to work.

People ask me if
the things in my
apartment are family
possessions, and
I say, "Yes, but not
my family."

— Mario Buatta

FAMILY

What's so great about being normal anyway?

Valerie, the girl who sat next to me in the fourth grade, had some exciting news one day. Our teacher asked her to share it. Valerie stood up and took a deep breath. "My granny is coming to live with us!" she said, beaming with pride, and promptly sat down.

My stomach lurched. A wave of deep melancholy shimmied up and down my nine-year-old spine. I have a hazy memory of turning to Valerie and, sotto voce, saying something like, "Oh, fucking hell. Well, look on the bright side. Maybe she'll die soon." Valerie stared back at me, lachrymose and ashen faced. I wanted Valerie's grandmother to die so Valerie could live. And Valerie, not unreasonably, now wanted me to die.

This was a teachable moment: it was my first exposure to the idea that relatives might be anything other than a source of wild-knuckled terror. In my defense, my warped idea about family was based on my reality. My childhood was spent bouncing between the schizophrenics in England and the alcoholics in Ireland. Relatives, my parents explained repeatedly, were a blight, always looking for handouts, needing to be institutionalized or bailed out of jail, offing themselves, or lacking the decency to die with enough money in a biscuit tin to cover the costs of their own interment.

When it came to relatives, Betty and Terry Doonan, my stoical, funny, brave parents, had been dealt a rough hand. How much easier their lives would have been if they had just swanned off in the other direction. Oh, look! Better people! Instead, they chose to wade into all the crap. They put roofs over relatives' heads. They weathered emotional cloudbursts and cleaned out grungy hovels. They understood that blood, even when diluted with vast quantities of booze, was thicker than water, and took care of flailing family members.

Flawed, deranged, fabulous, or freaky, your family members make you who you are—they are the primordial muck from which we all emerge.

The subtext of their actions was clear: We are the fruit of their crazy loins. We cannot let them shrivel and wither. Betty and Terry understood that cutting yourself off from family sets you adrift, leading to nihilism, sexual incontinence, masochistic behaviors, and self-destructive infatuations, or something like that. In other words, it's a lousy idea.

Radical Self-Care

Another lousy idea: martyrdom and self-denial. In order to survive your family, you also need to take care of yourself. If you subjugate yourself to the family psychodrama, you will end up tearing your wig off in a Tennessee Williams play of your own making and will never find yourself. Regardless of how freaky or fabulous your family, you need to dip in and out.

Even if yours is a storybook family, you will not become yourself unless you spread your wings and shake out the mothballs, roach motels, and Glade plug-ins.

My parents both took extended breaks from family. World War Two gave them a great excuse. They circled back on their folks a decade or two after the war ended, stronger and more mature, and began cleaning up the wreckage.

Like many gays I took an extended wellness break from my family. I kept them all at arm's length during my young adulthood. There was no mechanism for coming out back then. My gay secret was mine and mine alone. I needed to find out who I was and learn how to be my gay self.

Of her early dismal years, Coco Chanel supposedly said, "My life did not please me, so I created my life." This quotation exquisitely and perfectly—like a couture boucle suit—expresses how I dealt with my situation. My life, in my gritty small town, did not please me, so I began plotting and planning and imagining a better one. I took responsibility for creating my life.

The understanding that I was part of this strange, reviled group—blackmailed, entrapped, imprisoned, and shunned—was anxiety-producing but also set the wheels turning in my brain. It was the swinging '60s. The bleakness of my situation gave me an identity: crazy, bold, a total outsider. Instead of crumbling, I defiantly looked beyond the madhouse and the bottle-top factory to the twinkly lights of the metropolis— London was less than an hour away—where all the trendy people, the beautiful people in caftans with torrents of thick hair and kohl-rimmed eyes, were lounging about on circular beds with black satin sheets.

Unwitting Mentors

Betty and Terry were unconventional people who had a very clear sense of who they were. As a result, they attracted interesting characters into their circle of friends. I vividly recall time spent with these long-dead warriors of resilience:

BIRDSHIT

I was born in a rooming house. Lynn Burchett was our landlady. There was no way to say her name without it sounding like "Lynn Birdshit," so my parents gave up trying and just called her Birdshit, albeit affectionately. In her Tyrolean hiking boots and her Scottish kilt, burly Birdshit loomed large in our lives. She bred Afghan dogs, and she was the first, and quite possibly the only, person in Reading to own a futuristic bubble car. Her biggest claim to fame was her friendship with Marianne Faithfull's mother. When pop star Marianne started dating Mick Jagger, Lynn enjoyed the frisson of adjacent celebrity. And me? I nearly lost my mind. Swinging London was swinging low, sweet chariot, and I prayed that it would soon carry me (away from) home. It didn't. Not yet. After palling around with Mick and Marianne, Birdshit realized being called Birdshit might preclude her from joining the international jet set, so she changed her name to Lynette Saint Nicholas.

Lynn Burchett revealed to me the magical possibilities of personal rebranding.

I had quite a happy childhood growing up in Morristown, N.J. Looking back, I realize that some people are better suited for different phases in life. I was very good at being a child. I'm suited to have no real responsibility.

— Fran Lebowitz

ERIKA

My blind auntie, Phyllis, had several sightless friends, including Erika, a young German woman who had lost her vision while being tormented and starved in a Nazi concentration camp. Erika dressed like a little girl even though she was a young adult. She wore bows in her hair and white ankle socks with old-fashioned shoes. Since she was blind, I guess she had no way of assessing the effect her clothing had on others. I suspect this is how she was dressed when the soldiers took her away to the camps.

My sister and I, sarcastic ten year olds, used to laugh at her funny German accent and her attempts to speak English. When I told her I was about to take the eleven-plus exam—a notorious lengthy test that determined which kids would enjoy an enriching education at the grammar school (smiley face) and which kids should be shipped off to the "other" school where you left at sixteen and ended up at the bottle-top factory—Erika told me that she felt sure I would pass "with flying feathers" (*viz flyink fezzers*). My sister and I made fun of her for this malapropism, causing my mum to lose her sangfroid. "The bloody Krauts put her whole family up the chimney in Auschwitz, so I suggest you make an effort to be a lot nicer to her."

My sister and I were horrified and became much more solicitous toward her. When I failed the eleven-plus exam—with flying feathers—I could not help feeling it was a biblical punishment for taking the piss out of Erika. I made a point of not discussing it with her.

When all my pals and ex-boyfriends were dying horrible deaths from AIDS in the '80s, I often thought about Erika, and how she had stumbled, sightless and alone, out of the valley of death and, less than two decades later, was somehow capable of smiling and giving two shits about other people's kids and their stupid exams. Erika, the saddest, most poignant character I have ever met, taught me never to complain about my lot in life.

TONI

Toni gave me the greatest gift of all: she taught me how to be cheeky.

Antonia was one of my mum's friends. She was in her forties and had never married. She dressed like a Hungarian gypsy. I can still smell her heavy perfume and hear her jangly charm bracelets. She had a gravelly voice and a Welsh accent; she rolled her own cigarettes in a metal contraption, which she kept in her raffia purse. She was every inch herself, and, as a result, there was no shortage of blokes in her life. (See the "Love" chapter.)

One boyfriend owned a motorbike. Toni used to ride around on the back with her gypsy skirt flapping in the wind. She eventually fell off and, as a result, walked with a limp and a jeweled cane, which gave her the air of a retired ballet dancer.

One day Toni ran into me and my mum in the local high street.

"Betty! Luvvie! I've got a present for you," she declared, rummaging in her wicker basket and eventually pulling out a pineapple. My mum was taken aback. Pineapples were a rare sight in Reading in the early '60s.

"Oh! You shouldn't have," said my mum, which is what people said back then when they wanted to sound grateful.

"I wanted to show you my appreciation," said Toni, puffing on a freshly made ciggie, adding, "You are always so marvelous and kind."

At that moment, an acquaintance of Toni's walked by. She stopped to chat. Toni grabbed the pineapple from my mum and gave it to the other friend.

"Betty, darling! I want her to have it more than you. Do you mind?"

My mum did not take offense. She chalked it up to Toni's cheekiness.

These people: the Birdshits, the Erikas, the Tonis—random characters drawn into my parents' orbit—are often in my thoughts. The creation of yourself involves so much more than just your family tree. Strange, battered migrating birds will land on the outer branches, uninvited. Be sure to feed them a few worms and get to know them.

Siblings: Mentors or Tormentors?

I see siblings as functional items. What on earth is the point of siblings unless they are serving some kind of critical purpose? At the very least, they should provide some form of enthusiastic support system: I have decided to become a tennis pro, so I am going to need you to hit balls at me while crafting my off-court tabloid image.

My sister, Shelagh, and I are Irish twins. We were close in childhood. Our relationship was symbiotic and wildly transgendered. In fact, it was almost as if we had swapped DNA. She would toss her dollies in my direction. I would happily off-load any guns or trucks on her. I was Maid Marian to her Robin Hood. She liked westerns; I liked Busby Berkeley movies. Our childhood was a mixture of rollicking and mutual gender bending mixed with intense misery.

The misery started, ironically, when my dad got a job. Prior to this, unemployed Terry had been our nanny, diapering and feeding us in our squalid two-room attic flat, while Betty schlepped to find work.

Sis and I sporting gender-neutral handknits.

As an eight year old, my heroic dad had taken care of his two younger brothers through all kinds of dire circumstances. This is why he did such a bang-up job with my sister and me when we were infants. Caring for his younger siblings had equipped him with stellar nurturing skills.

So Betty and the now-employed Terry scoured the landscape for inexpensive daycare. They found it at the local public orphanage. This grim building, where we spent several years, was full of rage-filled war orphans and illegitimate children. Welcome to my Little Dorrit years. Since I have already dumped more than enough postwar austerity onto your plate, dear reader, I will spare you the details.

As we grew older, my sister and I began to lose track of each other. I focused on finding the glamorous caftan wearers and the satin sheet addicts with the abundant hair. Shelagh went in the polar (fleece) opposite direction, becoming an activist eco-lesbian. I was camp; she was woke. For several decades, we seemed to have nothing in common.

We reconnected in middle age, rekindling that childhood bond. We suddenly discovered that we had so much to talk about: that bloody orphanage, our fabulous mum and dad, sadistic schoolteachers, dropping pairs of granny's giant bloomers on her head from a top-floor window, and hiding Betty's dentures and then forcing her to recite the alphabet. (What a good sport she was! Like many of their generation, my parents wore dentures by their early thirties.) Sis and I were back to swapping dollies for trucks. She is now my favorite person on earth. We are very different. We created very different lives and selves. But we totally get each other.

Siblings serve multiple functions. They are so much more than just a place to dump off misgendered toys. They can also become cautionary tales. My husband feels strongly that his older siblings had a huge influence on how and when he chose to "set sail." He sums up the sibling relationship as follows: "By avoiding their shipwrecks, I charted my course." He was raised very far from the ocean in southern New Jersey and gets seasick if he even looks at a boat, so the seafaring metaphor is somewhat surprising.

Witting Mentors

While Erika et al. arrived in my life accidentally, there were others—many others over the years—who did not. I sought them out. I ransacked the universe to find them. They played an even bigger role in the development of my sense of self. I chose them.

The concept of chosen family is strongly associated with LGBTQ divas and warriors. In order to fully express ourselves, we marginalized people need to shift gears, often decamping to new locations, starting from scratch, and creating new tribes. We gays create the tribes of chosen family by hurling ourselves at like-minded souls. Hey, you! Wanna join?

I have a vast network of gay friends with whom I am sickeningly close. They know me better than any family member. We have all made the journey from fear and isolation to familial fabulosity. When I see them all lounging about in my living room, I feel completely happy, content, and accepted. Some of them wear caftans. I'm not sure if any of them have black satin sheets. I can think of a few who might. One thing is for sure: they are my beautiful people.

The concept of chosen family is not limited to the LGBTQ world. It is applicable to all and can play a key role in, per Coco Chanel, creating your life. In this regard, the gays offer a blueprint to every person who is on a vision quest to become their niftiest self: Don't be passive about creating your circle of life-enhancing superstars. Be picky, creative, and aggressive. Hurl yourself at like-minded souls. Get the family that you need.

Children

I do not have kids, but like many aging baby-boomer nonparents, I am an expert on parenting, with scads of

Call it a clan, call it a network, call it a tribe, call it a family. Whatever you call it, whoever you are, you need one.

— Jane Howard

vociferous opinions on the subject. Here goes: we live in an age in which kids and parents have anxious, neurotic relationships with each other. How can you be yourself, find yourself, create yourself when you are enmeshed with disempowering parents? Better to get thrown into a Dickensian orphanage every day than endure helicopter parenting.

Parents today seem overly involved in their children's lives. #collegeadmissionsscandal They even tattoo their kids' faces and names all over their bodies. It's a free country, but something about this desperate memorializing of your progeny smacks of ownership. By all means, tattoo your own name on your body—it will help with identification when you are found unconscious or dead in some inopportune circumstance.

The subtext of all this nannying is as follows: The world is a treacherous place. You cannot possibly navigate any aspect of reality without me breathing down your neck and orchestrating your journey. Without my oversight, you will be nothing. Surely all this excessive nannying inhibits a kid's ability to find, create, and unfurl themselves?

I got the opposite message. It can be summarized as follows: It's your life. Try not to fuck it up. My parents' only expectation of me was that I be able to pay my own bills once I reached adulthood. This you-figure-it-out approach allowed me to be myself from an early age.

Your dog thrives without helicopter parenting. Maybe your kid would, too.

How to Name Children

This is so much more profound than you might think. If contemporary parents spent as much time futzing with name selections as they do with college applications, the world would be a better place. Or, at the very least, a place where everyone on earth had a noteworthy name.

You might as well give your kid a memorable name with a sense of grandeur. The kid can always change it later if he/she/they starts to feel upstaged by it. Jermaine Jackson named his child Jermajesty Jackson. Jermajesty has yet to switch out his name. Hopefully, he will keep it. David Bowie named his first child Zowie Bowie. The kid later changed his name to Joey and then to Duncan. I bet you anything he goes back to Zowie Bowie at some point. Zowie will be great in the senior home: hey, Zowie, another round of canasta?

Mr. and Mrs. Bowie and their son, Zowie.

In my experience, if people start to feel that their given name does not match their emerging self, they will happily rename themselves. Betty Doonan's real name was Martha. She loathed it because it was too frumpy. The name Betty better expressed her film-noir essence. In a stunning coincidence, our dog Foxylady's shelter name was also Martha. We changed it to Foxylady for the same reason my mother changed hers to Betty: it better expressed her sassy *je ne sais quoi*.

The naming of dogs tends to be spontaneous and unconstipated. When, in 2019, Harry and Meghan named their boy Archie, they won our hearts. It was as if they threw five hundred years of encumbering European history out the window and gave him a dachshund name.

I recognize that my circumstances—the orphanage, dentures, bubble cars, and lunatic fringes—were more extreme than those experienced by the average reader.

I had a brother who was my savior, made my childhood bearable. He was older by five years, Jack Sendak... he took his time with me to draw pictures and read stories and live a kind of fantastical life.

— Maurice Sendak

How should seekers hailing from less Dickensian familial situations set about the task of navigating family dynamics? How should you go about trying to be yourself if you were born into, for example, pampered luxury?

Richesse and privilege are no guarantee of happiness—usually the opposite. Life gets more complicated the more stuff you have. Number one tip: stop whining. I find that the amount of complaining today is completely deafening. The less people have to kvetch about, the more they kvetch. If you live with your family in Brentwood and you feel oppressed and put upon, go spend a week in downtown Mogadishu and get back to me. Constant whingeing does not help you become your most fabulous self. Stop focusing on obstacles and speed bumps and develop a dramatically exaggerated sense of possibility. Once you have stopped complaining and are engorged with your new sense of possibility, then...grab the menu and start ordering.

Regardless of your background, your family's various traits and predispositions form a menu—two menus, in fact. You can pick and choose your entrees and your side dishes from either parent, based on your own needs and circumstances. You have the advantage of being able to see how things played out. You can emulate your mum's vigorous creativity but recoil from your dad's grumpy antipathy toward housework. You can cultivate granny's green thumb or emulate Uncle Vince's visionary business acumen. From superficial to profound, the options are extensive. (Like a massive laminated IHOP menu.)

I have seen what booze can do to people, so I avoid alcohol. More terrifying still, I have also seen the havoc that can be wrought by wearing pastel-hued stretch velour tracksuits and reacted accordingly. So grab your lorgnette and take a moment to read that family menu. Linger over the descriptions of the main courses and fine wines. And then snap your fingers (metaphorically, because nobody in their right mind does that anymore) for the waiter. Bon appétit!

CONCLUSION

Deep Thoughts and a Few Shallow Ones

You have just read an entire book that encourages you to focus on, introspect about, maximize, floss, and fluff yourself. It has been a very productive interlude. You have barked like a Labrador dog, scored a new job with unlimited kale chips, dated a flopped soufflé, repopularized scrunchies, and developed a dramatic new signature walk. You have found outlets for self-expression in the boudoir, the office cubicle, and the gym. In the pursuit of personal authenticity, you have left no hairdresser unturned. Armed with a new sense of self, you are now ready to take the ultimate challenge. The time has come to put down that mirror, to pivot, and to unself.

Some philosophers feel that pivoting away from the self is the key to contentment. Iris Murdoch (she of the bowl haircut in the "Style" chapter) labeled this notion "unselfing." After "selfing" your way through this entire book, it would only be good manners to give unselfing a whirl. Unselfing is more than just not taking selfies for a couple of hours. But, don't fret, it is fairly straightforward. First, you must focus on turning your attention outward, away from yourself and onto your surroundings. The goal of unselfing is to see things as they really are rather than through the lens of your selfish trifles. Sometimes the act of unselfing involves people. It can also involve works of art and nature.

One day, Dame Iris found herself looking out the window in an agitated frame of mind, "brooding perhaps on some damage done to my prestige." (For Murdoch "the fat relentless ego" is our biggest foe.) She spied a hovering bird of prey, and bam, everything changed. The emotional pain evaporated. The falcon became the focus.

Unselfing in the Murdoch sense is about so much more than bird-watching. It is the key to love and life and culture. A noteworthy passage from Murdoch's essay "The Sublime and the Good" explains it best: "Love is the extremely difficult realization that something other than oneself is real. Love, and so art and morals, is the discovery of reality."

I'm not trying to sell you me, I'm trying to sell you, you.

— Lizzo

It would be a catastrophic mistake to conclude that your selfing journey has been a waste of time. Selfing is a very necessary precursor to unselfing. So now that you have successfully selfed and unselfed, what's next? "Collective effervescence!" That's what's next.

There I was flipping through *National Geographic* when I came upon a life-changing article titled "Karma of a Crowd," by Laura Spinney. She described a phenom called collective effervescence in which a special energy arises when a group of people feels a strong sense of shared identity and reverence. Social scientists had studied millions of worshippers gathering along the Ganges for religious festivals. Despite the perilous and cold conditions, lack of food, and bacteria-riddled water, pilgrims reported a sense of improved health.

As you may well have gathered, I am an extremely skeptical self-help guru. When it comes to hippie-dippy stuff—transcendentalism, mysticism, etc.—I am the first one to call bullshit. In the instance of collective effervescence, however, I am, based on the level of social science research and the astounding size of the statistical samples, completely sold. The data blew my man bag clean off my shoulder. I am a believer in the magic of collective effervescence.

Down by the Ganges, the power of the group defied objective scientific expectations. Instead of becoming sick, worshippers left the festival feeling renewed and rather fabulous. The throng melted into a state of unity, and the collective effervescence created a mysterious positive energy that impacted physiology in measurable scientific ways. To quote Spinney, "a throng of millions can become one." (When I read this article all I could think was, "No wonder people in L.A. get depressed, isolated in their cars. No wonder they go tearing off to the green market or a NASCAR race. They are desperate for a hit of collective effervescence.")

Your takeaway: finding yourself, being yourself is great. Thumbs up! Congratulations. And, having solidified the dimensions of your self, you can now unself, whenever the mood strikes. Look skyward! Is that a hovering falcon or just an elegant pigeon? It matters not. Either one will help you pivot from your own *mishegas* to the majesty of the wider world.

And every now and then, take time to gird up your newly actualized loins and collectively effervesce with other selves in a ritualized moment of transcendental joie de vivre—a rave, a knitting circle, a Soul Train line, a 10K, a meatless mahjong meetup—and lose yourself in the trance and the prance and the kiki.

Sound good?

The slow and steady evolution of *moi*.

The whole problem
is to establish
communication with
one's self.

— E. B. White

GLOSSARY

Badinage: witty, scintillating chitchat.

Balaclava: cold-weather head-covering with minimal face exposure. #sinister

Boiserie: ornate wooden carving. (French)

Bris: Jewish ceremony of circumcision.

Court shoes: conservative low-heeled shoes, appropriate for wearing to court, whether legal or royal.

Crepe de chine: dress fabric produced either with all-silk warp and weft or with a silk warp and hard-spun worsted weft. Very '30s but also '70s. It has a definite slink to it. (French)

Duds: clothes. When applied to clothing, this is a neutral term and does not imply negative judgment. When applied to a bloke, it suggests that the individual in question is fundamentally lacking in some important but unspecified way.

Goujon: small strip of fish or chicken deep-fried in breadcrumbs. A fancy way of saying McNuggets. (French)

Grande horizontale: a lady who makes her living in the boudoir, presumably in a horizontal position. (French)

Irish Exit: practice of leaving an event without notifying others.

Kagool: weatherproof hooded garment. (British)

Kiki: gathering of friends for the purpose of gossiping and chitchat. An expression brought to a wider audience by the song "Let's Have a Kiki" by the Scissor Sisters and by RuPaul's *Drag Race*. Also a verb.

Kvell: to feel happy and proud. Example: "Mindy got into Stanford! I'm kvelling!" (Yiddish)

Kvetchers: complainers. People who kvetch. (Yiddish)

Lorgnette: pair of glasses or opera glasses held in front of a person's eyes by a long handle on one side. Very eighteenth century. Very camp. (French)

Mishegas: madness/confusion. (Yiddish)

Mouchoir: handkerchief. (French)

Mumsy: matronly and frumpy. (British)

Naff: pedestrian, dreary, and unstylish. (British)

Paillette: large sequin. (French)

Poule de luxe: trophy wife, high-class hooker, or just somebody who enjoys luxury. *Poule* = hen. (French) See also *grande horizontale*.

Sansculottes: Literally "those without knee breeches." A label applied to the militant, ragged, ruthless supporters of the French Revolution, especially between 1792 and 1795. (French)

Sashay away: popularized by RuPaul and understood to indicate that speedy departure—*hit the road, buster!*— is advisable.

Scrummy: popular abbreviation of scrumptious. (British)

Scuffies: fluffy bedroom slippers. #cozy (British)

Shekel: monetary unit in ancient and contemporary Israel.

Slag off: to speak negatively of others or things. (British)

SO: significant other, aka partner.

Sturm und Drang: literal meaning: storm and stress. (German)

Szhoosh: Festoon (verb). Fabric or foliage that is deployed in the act of szhooshing (noun). (Doonan)

Tussy: posh, fancy, and deluxe, as in Park Avenue or Beverly Hills. The opposite of grungy. Inspired by Tussy, a '70s cream deodorant, and was first used as an adjective by writer Mayer Rus back in the '90s. Not widely used, but very useful, just like the product.

Twee: encumbered with a ditzy, granny aesthetic.

Wallabees: moccasin-inspired '70s suede lace-up ankle boots.

Weltschmerz: painful feeling of melancholy and world-weariness. (German)

Whingeing: kvetching. (British)

Woggle: circular device used to anchor a scout or girl-guide neckerchief. Think napkin ring. (British)

Yenta: gossip or busybody, with a penchant for matchmaking. (Yiddish)

PICTURE CREDITS

Phaidon Press Limited
2 Cooperage Yard
London E15 2QR

Phaidon Press Inc.
65 Bleecker Street
New York, NY 10012

phaidon.com

First published 2020
© 2020 Phaidon Press Limited

ISBN 978 1 83866 141 0

A CIP catalogue record for this book is
available from the British Library and
the Library of Congress.

Project Editor: Sara Bader
Design: Hans Stofregen
Production Controllers: Abigail Draycott
and Lily Rodgers

Printed in Italy